To Dora Guerra,
a good fan,
a new Book,
with warm wishes —

Shelby Hearon

San Antonio
June 18, 1981

PAINTED
DRESSES

PAINTED DRESSES

Shelby Hearon

Atheneum 1981 New York

Excerpts from "Mamie," "Fellow Citizens," "Mag," and "Mill-Doors" by
Carl Sandburg from THE COMPLETE POEMS OF CARL SANDBURG, published
by Harcourt Brace Jovanovich, Inc., are reprinted by permission.

The excerpt from "The Lake Isle of Innisfree" from COLLECTED POEMS
of William Butler Yeats (Copyright 1906 by Macmillan Publishing Co.,
Inc., renewed 1934 by W. B. Yeats), is reprinted by permission.

The excerpt from "Song, I Am Tired to Death" from COLLECTED POEMS
of James Stephens (Copyright 1912 by Macmillan Publishing Co., Inc.,
renewed 1940 by James Stephens), is reprinted by permission.

Library of Congress Cataloging in Publication Data

Hearon, Shelby, ——
    Painted dresses.

    I. Title.
PS3558.E256P3 1981   813'.54   80-69644
ISBN 0-689-11155-X

Copyright ©1981 by Shelby Hearon
All rights reserved
Published simultaneously in Canada by McClelland and Stewart Ltd.
Composition by American–Stratford Graphic Services, Brattleboro,
    Vermont
Manufactured by Fairfield Graphics, Fairfield, Pennsylvania
Designed by Mary Cregan
First Edition

CONTENTS

To know how to question means to know how to wait, even a whole lifetime. But an age which regards as real only what goes fast and can be clutched with both hands looks on questioning as "remote from reality" and as something that does not pay, whose benefits cannot be numbered. But the essential is not number; the essential is the right time, the right moment, and the right perseverance.

—MARTIN HEIDEGGER

1

Kansas City
Train Station

Nell

IT IS HARD TO TELL what something you are part of is really like; it is the way you cannot see a picture if you are in it looking out.

Nell was a brown girl in a heavy brown coat in a brown train station; halfway between the aunts and their hardwoods and strange yellow daylight and stories of happy baby days, and Mommy's house of pink stucco with its pink flamingos and stories of Nell's happy marriage to come.

The aunts kept their eggs in the wrong place, and took her up a frosty hill to pick blackberries, which weren't in season, and told her anecdotes about some cousin raking leaves the winter Papa got angina. Theirs was a world uncertain beneath its surface.

The aunts were older than age, ancient Sears and Roebuck copies of genteel ladies, their paint and powder cracked and dried on their wrinkled skin. Vinnie had shoe-black dyed hair pulled tight in a waxy bun, a gashed red mouth, dark circles under her eyes, behind spectacles making darker circles. This aunt was always belted, buttoned, serviceable, wearing the dark blue of austerity. The other, Minnie, appeared voluptuous even in her seventies, in her purple voiles, flowered lawns, with her fleshy breasts above an antique cameo. She had carmine hair and orangey lips arched over powdered crinkles of cheek, and fixed staring eyes like an old doll's.

Strangely enough, it was Minnie who had been the old maid sister; Vinnie who had married and carried the still-born child. It had been both who later raised their deceased brother's only girl.

It was this niece, Estelle (Nell's mother), who started the rhyming. As a child she had dismissed the aunts' earlier names and rechristened them Vinnie and Minnie. Later, when her own daughters came along, she called them La-Nelle and Moselle so that she and they would make triplets. Then, after she'd shed the little girls' daddy and found a pink rich stepfather for them, she had rhymed her own a second time: "This is your new Papa, dears, and his name is Tommy Woodard. You can call us Mommy and Tommy, won't that be fun?"

The inside of the aunts' house was as confusing to Nell now as the name change had been to her then. As you would expect of women their age with time and breeding to occupy them, they liked order. There were black, stacked boxes of winter blankets and summer shoes. And boxes for church hats, out-of-season coats, lace, bows, belts, and bouquets pressed between tissue paper. Under-neath all that was what you did not anticipate.

Nell, looking behind the bathroom door for some toilet paper, had found twenty-four Mason jars of jams and jel-lies. (She had used her underpants to dry between her legs.) Another day she had looked in the vegetable bin for an apple; and seen instead a dozen crocus bulbs. Early one morning, hoping to fix herself breakfast before the aunts were up to make a morning of it, she had found sewing

4

machine bobbins nesting in the egg carton cups.

In the kitchen things were arranged by appearance and not by use: white powders sat side by side in tins, cake flour, roach killer, boric acid. Three identical glass shakers held white crystals: sugar, salt, and one Nell did not know and did not want to taste. Grapenuts sat in a well-sealed jar next to peppercorns.

The aunts were dismayed by her confusion. "What is it, child?"

"She's upset with us, Vinnie."

"Whatever for? We had ham and sweet potatoes—"

"She wanted an egg, she says, for breakfast. I don't know why she couldn't have waited until we got up, now do you? We've been feeding her just fine, a big strapping girl like her."

"I couldn't find the eggs, Aunt Minnie."

"Why, we keep them in that plant stand by the window. They do better at room temperature, dear. Didn't Estelle teach you that? Cold eggs make cakes fall, as everyone knows."

"The bobbins in the refrigerator?"

"Sew better cold. Thread doesn't stick, so we use the icebox."

"Refrigerator, sister."

"Refrigerator."

"Why are the jams in the bathroom?" Nell asked.

"Homes used to have cellars, LaNelle, before your day. When we had coal-burning furnaces down here, and you needed a dark place to store your canning—light spoils things you know—you used the cellar."

"Where do you keep the toilet paper?" Nell blushed.

"The bathroom tissue, dear, is with all the paper goods in the front hall closet. Why didn't you just come tell us you were out? We keep the paper goods all together so we can check at a glance on what's running low when we go out the door on the way to the store."

How reasonable it seemed when explained in their way.

One afternoon they took Nell on a climb through the bare hardwoods above the old Springs Hotel, and both ladies had damp eyes over earlier days. They forgot, in their remembering, that you cannot pick blackberries between Christmas and New Year's, when the grass is brittle with frost, and a wind is blowing.

Nell pieced together the reason for the cold return to a hillside in the past. In their youth, some summer, they had both fallen in love with a second cousin once removed who had taken the train down from Louisville to the Baths. At that time the mineral water spa had a steady clientele who came from as far as St. Louis and New Orleans, enticed by the brochure (now on Aunt Minnie's wall, in ornate frame) that claimed: "For many of the female diseases it affords a permanent remedy, and, for the gentlemen, frog shooting, billiards, fine riding, and, for all, at the table, fresh Jersey milk, spring chickens, and other delicacies of the rural table." Vinnie and Minnie (then Vanessa and Mineola) took the cousin in hand—and no one else ever got a chance at him. The story went that he had danced with Minnie and maybe held her hand, or more, but that the afternoon of the blackberry picking he had proposed instead to Vinnie. It might have been a mistake; it might not. He had lived, at any rate, with both of them until his untimely death. And if it was Minnie who got quavery over "our dear husband" and had to dab her eyes and heave her breasts, it may not have been the greater sorrow but the larger accoutrements for showing it. Or so Nell reconstructed it.

6

"You must tell Estelle we brought you to the Springs. She'll want to know. She loved to come here as a little thing, and run all over the place. Do you remember, sister, when she scratched her knees on all the thorns?"

"You and your sister Moselle were lucky little girls to have a mother like our Estelle, now weren't you?"

Nell looked about at the slopes where berries had once been, and took in the strong smell of black walnut husks, and saw down below them a dense grapevine in a dark hollow. The outside was good. The light seemed yellow to her. She had not remembered that from before, not consciously. When you were little you did not know what you knew.

Inside, at the aunts' house, the rooms were tightly ordered into blocks of color. The Red Room, Aunt Minnie's room, had Victorian flocked wallpaper; all, the walls, rug, draperies, and bedspreads, were in suffocating reds of deep ruby and bright vermilion.

Aunt Vinnie's, on the other hand, was blue, a soured, blank blue, a watered blue, on love seats and pleated spreads and striped walls, that turned to gray in the late afternoon. The Yellow Room was the harsh color of egg yolks cooked too long; it was a late addition to the house, once a screened porch where Never, the maid, churned milk, and Almost, the gardener, took off his hat and wiped the sweat while doing yard work. Upstairs under the eaves was the Green Room, for guests, with ivied paper and latticed windows.

Nell's favorite was the parlor, the Rose Room, with its dusty rose the shade of dried flowers and a dusty green for their stems, and rose-scented sachets, and vases of tea roses and laurel leaves made of silk. On the mantle was placed an arrangement of white china roses. A fragile, translucent white, they did not belong. They were not the *color* rose; but the *name* rose. Capodimonte the aunts called them;

7

a name that meant white mountain, or top of the mountain, Nell wasn't sure. They were the color of snow. They belonged in a white marble house in Italy with quarry-tile floors and white balustrades on balconies that looked out on a view of a lake as static as the mirror behind them. Or they belonged, instead, in the nursery, the White Room. The Babies Room.

Nell had not wanted to stay in the Babies Room this visit.

"If you don't like the nursery, dear," Minnie had responded the first night, "we can always put you up in the Green Room upstairs. We keep that for the cousins from Louisville; we keep their things in the drawers, so they will feel at home. I keep the sheets changed fresh for them, as they're so nice to have us come up for garden tour and the Derby. We just can't do enough. But we let Estelle and her Tommy have it when they came; and so can you, too, of course. It isn't a lot of trouble . . ."

"She always liked the nursery," Vinnie had countered, settling it for them. "You always liked the nursery, didn't you? You were happier there than at any time in your life. I remember. You were lucky little girls growing up here."

Nell remembered it differently.

The first time her stepfather bothered her she had been playing a game with Mo, who was a baby of two. Nell was inside, peeking through the white curtains at Mo, who was hunting for her in the back yard. While she watched, Tommy came in and closed the door. "Hiya, hon," he said. (Or whatever he said in those days. Maybe that was what he said now in Texas. Maybe then he said, "Hello, little darling." She could not remember.) With his thatch of dyed yellow hair stiff as straw and his pink cheeks he looked like a play actor and not a real daddy.

8

He stretched out on the bed and held four-year-old Nell high over his head, and laughed the way adults did when they were not really laughing. "I'll tell you a story." She had on a brown cotton dress, and one of the white organdy pinafores that Mommy liked to keep on her little girls. She had on white panties, which Tommy put his hand into from behind as he lowered her on top of him. The stiff thing under her stomach made a ridge from between her legs to her navel as he rocked her gently back and forth across it, while he felt into the crease of her behind with his fingers. "Once upon a time," he said, holding her down with his hand, putting his pink face against hers.

It was a long time before he let her go, and by then Mo, outside, had cried herself to sleep by the back porch with a neighbor's dog beside her. They had her in the house and down for a nap when Mommy and the aunts got home from Garden Club, and Never arrived to start supper, and Almost, who had been raking the front, said he was done for the day.

Those things happened. It did not have to matter now, fifteen years later. Now, Nell would like to have had the white roses in the White Room, where they belonged.

"Will you leave me the Capodimonte?" she had asked the aunts, not thinking a mention of their departure would offend ladies in their seventies.

"Child, there's time enough for that when I'm cold. I don't want to be like our cousin who has every piece in her home marked—turn it up end and look at the bottom, some name taped right there."

"You can't take it with you, sister."

"That doesn't mean you let them carve on you like a turkey still warm."

"I think we could save them for you, LaNelle. Unless

they are dear to your mother. Estelle, you know, is all the family we have left. Our poor brother's child. Our own, you know, never lived."

Two years after the time Mo cried herself to sleep on the back porch, their pink stepdaddy received the first dividends on his far off oil leases, and moved them all to Texas. Mommy was delighted; the stay at the aunts' had never been intended as anything but temporary chaperoned quarters from which to move from one husband to the next.

They left on an Easter Sunday. Easter was Mommy's ultimate production. There were burnished eggs, gilded lilies, tinted icings; there were raw reds, stale yellows, blank blues, acrid oranges. Mommy put decals of hens and bunnies and posies, gummy and blurred, on all the damp shells that weren't going to make chickens. (The aunts explained: they never bought eggs that could hatch. But sometimes an egg would have a bloody fuzzy scrap of a thing inside when they opened it for breakfast, and they would scream and return it to the store. Nell's mother's eggs, however, were full of hardboil instead.)

Each year there were photographs of little Nell and Mo in lavender gabardine suits with violet pongee blouses and yellow cotton socks and gloves. Each year a snapshot showed Nell growing taller and farther away from the top of Mo's head. (Too tall. In later, Texas, pictures, you could see Nell's knees bent, buckling in apology for towering over the smaller sister, and then even over the diminutive mother. In turn, you could see Mo each year straining on tiptoe to catch up—bursting with that big grin that made a second daughter acceptable.) It was pathetic: that anxious lavender, the Easter sun making squints in their anticipating eyes.

10

That last Easter in Kentucky Nell had stolen four eggs, still warm from boiling, not yet colored. She had carried them into the white nursery and put them on the sheet where baby Mo slept. (She was told that once there had been a third baby on the way, but it had got lost in castor oil after Mommy met Tommy Woodard.) At bedtime, Mo had climbed up into bed and squashed the eggs. But she didn't cry or tell on Nell to Mommy or the aunts. Trusting her big sister, she had trudged along behind her in the dark while they flushed the eggs down the white commode.

Nell sat in a brown coat, brown plaid skirt, brown loafers, brown hair tied back with a brown grosgrain ribbon. She knew she looked drab, and a student. But she was.

The train station also was drab: wood benches, brown and black marble floors, black radiators, a vast ceiling meant to be grand but dingy from years of burning coal. She looked around her. There were three old men wearing black cloth coats and black beards, with skull caps on their heads, rubbing their hands together as if before a fire. There were two graying women whose veined hosed legs below gray overcoats straddled shopping bags as they nodded toward one another wordlessly. One white nun, colorless as ashes, sat apart both in space and by decision.

A college boy about her age walked through the gate marked ARRIVALS. Something about him made her think of the white roses in the Rose Room. It was his sweater. It was wrong. He had on a loud red sweater with three reindeer on it. It was *bright;* and he was *bright,* you could tell. But he had mistaken one meaning of the word for the other, and so he didn't fit with himself. He was subdued, and his face looked as if he were far away studying something inside his head.

Nell looked toward her own gate: DEPARTURES. She too was thinking. She did not know what happened to the bothered bed and Easter eggs and squinting afternoons when they were over and inside you. She did not know if they showed through.

If you were in the picture, all you could see was out.

Nick

——◆——

NICHOLAS CLARK dreaded his return home.

He was not the sort of person who would have, or could have, stolen his brother's girl. He had feet that splayed out, and ears that protruded. But the fact was he had done so; had got engaged to the girl his brother had brought home to meet the family last summer. It did not matter that this exchange had taken place after Richard had done with her, and without apparent rancor. He knew Richard; there would be some toll extracted.

Anyone named for a British king who called his dog Wat Tyler after the leader of a squashed revolt so that he could kick him around and who wired the rose bushes so that his dog was half electrocuted every time he lifted a leg to pee, anyone with such a mindset would get his revenge.

Richard had been getting even with Nicholas since they were boys. At first covertly, and then, from the time of the gold birthday party, wholly out in the open.

Prior to that event, he and Richard, born a year and a week apart, had always had joint celebrations. These events took place, and Nicholas had always accepted their form and occurrence without question. A week or so before the party, Richard would tell him that their mother had said that this year it was all right to ask all the boys in the class, or that girls could come too, and that it would be a scavenger hunt, or, if Easter was early, perhaps an egg hunt. And Nicholas would go along, assuming that the word came from his mother. The birthdays would come off, and their mother would preside in one of her flowered dresses that went with public mothering, ribbons caught in her hair, even an eyelet apron, and afterwards she would say to the boys' father that this year she had put on the best party that the boys had ever had. And he would say that it had the special air that one looked for in any entertaining by Mary Ann Clark.

The year Nicholas was eleven, all that changed. He was still waiting for instructions to be spelled out as to whom to invite when an afternoon arrived before the usual date and, with it, all of Richard's friends from his class. A gold cake appeared, and golden streamers that led to such places as the old well, and the attic stairs, and the cistern on the hill above the railroad yards, where prizes had been concealed. And Nicholas had known nothing of it. His mother was embarrassed for him. "But dear, didn't you want to have any friends? When we talked, I thought, your brother—"

Nicholas stood there at the party, ears out, not understanding. When had any of this been discussed? When was a date set? Had Richard always guided their mother's ramblings and then in the end done it all himself? Who ordered the cake? Who bought the streamers, prizes, favors? He recalled other years being handed little cards to pass out at school, sometimes by Richard, sometimes by his mother. Where had they come from?

"What happened to you, son?" his father asked.

What happened was that he saw that he was on his own. Richard had declared every man for himself.

Now, by marrying Virginia, Nicholas would deliver yet another weapon into his brother's hands.

But he felt he had no choice. He was not selecting her; she had been selected for him by the fantasy of his twelve-year-old mind.

It began ten years ago, on an evening when his grandfather and father talked alone over cigars in the library. It was peacetime, and they told war stories; and then his grandfather told a tale from the First World War, of having seen passages beneath the city of London where certain gentlemen kept women who never saw the light of day but who were kept secluded in luxury for the uses of pleasure. What they dwelt on, the father and grandfather, were the tattoos that adorned these women's breasts. Why, his grandfather had asked his son, a doctor, would a woman endure needles in that delicate area, for what vanity? They debated at length the degree of pain involved in etching one delicate butterfly above a nipple.

Nicholas could not imagine it. He longed to see it; the woman scream, then heal, then show her ornamented breast. It lodged in him a desire that would not go away: for such a woman, willing to be branded for you. His fantasies from that time formed a life separate from his at school. Self-conscious about his ears and feet, he dated little in high school, and even in college. What dates he had did not in any way connect with the tattooed woman in his solitary underground.

Richard had not heard the London story, and Nicholas did not share it; but by the osmosis of siblings, Richard had sensed this special weakness of his plodding brother. He must have.

Why else would he have sent Virginia to him?

Richard had gone with her all last summer and then brought her home to meet his parents; she was the one after Patty and the one before Kathy. She was pretty, and had heavy ankles that did not seem to go with the rest of her but gave her a languid way of moving. She wore her hair curly, and long gored skirts, and clinging sweaters over breasts that seemed too low and loose for such a young girl. She seldom talked. She didn't appear to notice Nicholas at all; and Richard's parents were a mystery to her. It was as if she had an off switch and an on switch, and did not bother to dissemble. Nicholas felt comfortable with her when she was off, because her lack of concern did not seem to require anything of him.

The last night she was at the house, when he was almost asleep, she had come into his room.

He leapt out of bed, startled. It was clear she had been with Richard and not in the guest room at the far end of the house as she was supposed to be. He was surprised at that. And at her appearing in a lavender gown that showed clearly her low breasts and rounded stomach.

"Richard said to show you," she said, closing the door softly. She moved toward him until he could see on her right shoulder the small tattoo of a butterfly.

He blinked his eyes, and then he reached out and touched it. "Did it hurt?" he asked.

"Sure, some." She shrugged, showing it off in the gesture which made her strap slip down.

He did not know what to do.

"He told me to show you." She moved off indifferently on her heavy legs, closing the door behind her as she left.

In September Richard wrote his brother in Cambridge that he had dumped Virginia; he was seeing Kathy. In

October Nicholas called Richard to ask if he could write Virginia and invite her for a weekend at school.

"Why not?" Richard had retorted. "I'll roadtest them all for you, if you like, brother. You can retread those you want."

Then, Thanksgiving, when they were both home for vacation, Richard had presented his brother with a cur dog he said was named Boris for someone Czar Nicholas had suppressed. To kick around. "As long as you're following in your brother's footsteps, you might as well go all the way."

Nicholas had taken the dog to the pound.

Richard always did what seemed unexpected, yet which was on one level the most obvious behavior. Their father's family, the Clarks, were from New England, thinkers who had stood firmly in the path of each new idea that came along, opposing in turn Darwin, Marx, and Freud. Each male forebear in the family until their father had finished at Harvard and gone into scholarship. Their father's failure to make it there had shaped his life: he had finished at Chicago, and subsequently chosen to settle in the vast middle-classed midwest, to live out his life a medical doctor, as if in exile.

His eldest, Nicholas, was trained to carry on the family tradition from the start. There was an often-repeated legend of Nicholas asking his father: "How do I know I'm not dreaming?" And being for months afterwards barraged with lectures by his father on Appearance and Reality, on John Stuart Mill and his brilliance and breakdown, and on Nicholas' own precosity and what he must do with his life. He was four at the time.

Needless to say, when the time came he went to Harvard and did well. Richard, however, had retaliated against all that by going one better. Instead of doing what his father preached, he did what his father practiced: he went to Chicago.

(In some ways he was more like their mother. Listening to her was like watching a ball of twine unravel across the floor. The difference was, Richard knew what he was unwinding.)

If the fact of not making it at Harvard was central to their father's life, the fact of not being Russian was the core of their mother's. While still in college she had discovered that although her brothers had been born to their Russian mother, a fabled beauty of the nobility, she had not. She had been the only child of her father and a woman who had died while she was quite small. Growing up she had idolized this supposed mother who had fled the homeland, one of the many White Russians carrying their titles and belongings in valises across the border, seeking exile in new countries. She did not get over the news; she refused to accept it. The photograph album shows a young woman with small feet shod in boots that suggest more bitter winters than those in Kansas.

As their father related it to Nicholas and Richard years before, Mary Ann's father had not wanted to die with his secret and so wrote her the truth. Their mother herself never alluded to it, except that it was the roadblock she stumbled over in all her ramblings.

Only once in his life had Nicholas ever seen anyone confront her directly.

Nicholas was in high school, and Mary Ann was entertaining visitors, two men, older, whom the boys did not know. She wore her wine velvet suit with narrow pants and satin blouse: her company suit that suggested a European salon. Nicholas had grown to dread such evenings, but he did not yet admit it, except to the extent that he hated the moment when the company would have to hear again the story of himself at four asking: "How do I know I'm not dreaming?"

That night the older of the two visitors, a Dr. Cavender, had admired and asked about the carved mahogany table behind the little sofa.

"My father," their mother began softly, touching her trouser legs, "had it made for his second wife, who was not my mother, actually, but the Russian woman I grew up thinking I was descended from, which, I suppose, as far as rearing goes, because of all the things in my father's house, which he brought from his younger brother, oddly enough, as in those days it was the custom for the elder to have university and the younger to have trade, as they liked to say, themselves having done fairly well at both, so that there was no need for competition there, although the fact of my being a girl was helpful, as girls at that time were expected to choose between trade and university only as pertained to husband, of course, not as pertained to furthering either herself, or the family. You see—?" She smiled, then, and spread her small hands in a disarming gesture to show their openness, that nothing had been concealed from the listener. "And in my case I have certainly never regretted the choice," she concluded, looking at her husband.

Then Frank, the boys' father, rose and kissed her cheek in a way that indicated everyone would feel that she had said something direct and charming. And then he waited, as on every other such occasion, for someone present to lean back in his chair and pick out some thread from her narrative and begin a story of his own. Which might deal with younger and older brothers, education versus commerce, real and stepparents, any number of topics. That was how Mary Ann Clark's evenings went.

This time, after the kiss from Frank, after Mary Ann had fluttered her hands and smiled, and Richard had yawned behind her head, Dr. Cavender said: "You started to tell us about the mahogany table, Marian?"

"My father made it . . . for his first wife . . ." She had looked frightened. "Who was not . . ." She was asking how much of all that he wanted to hear again. Her face asked where she was supposed to start, had she not navigated the journey from table safely past the one who was not her mother but said she was? Surely she could not be expected to do it again.

"Did you have some especial interest in the table, sir?" Frank assumed a chilly tone.

"What? No. I was merely curious. The carving caught my eye."

"Then I should think my wife had quite sufficiently recounted—?"

"Quite." The dark man turned to his companion with a change in topic.

After the guests had left, their father moved to sit beside their mother with a glass of brandy. "Don't let Cavender unsettle you, dear heart. I should have warned you that he is a psychoanalyst just come to the treatment hospital. I should have thought to warn you they can be quite foolish in an ordinary evening's conversation."

"He was amusing," Mary Ann answered brightly. "Here I was giving him everything that Sigmund Freud could ask for, an intimate glimpse of my father and mother, although she wasn't actually, at any rate, how droll, he asks about the table instead, is he, do you think, repressing his Mummy . . ." She turned to her husband so that they might share the laugh.

20

"We're going to bed, boys, and it's time you did, also." Their father said goodnight.

"Now, dear, let's be circumspect and say that we're going up to discuss table . . ." She smiled and put her arm through his, brushing aside Dr. Cavender's unsettling visit.

No wonder Nicholas dreaded going home. It was not only Richard; it was the pair of them, his parents, forever smiling in the library.

How different Virginia's house in Cleveland had been. How incredibly different. If he had adored her before, for her face that turned on for him, and off for others, and for her slow-moving legs and low breasts and tiny pinpoints on her shoulder, and the fact that there was such a short distance between the start of her sentences and their ends, he had loved her the more for her fussy house and grandparents.

Even the beaded curtain.

Cleveland, where he had not been before, was a dirty, bitter-cold city with Russian and Greek church spires, a frozen waterway, and working people. Virginia had told him that her father was a doctor like his. This was true, technically, but the fact was that she had not seen her father since she was born. She had said it thinking to impress him, just as she had told her grandparents that his was, and that he might become one, too. She knew better, but studies of the brain had no frame of reference in their thinking, as she explained to him.

The grandmother was a large woman who had also raised Virginia's two older sisters, and was anxious to have this last one gone, and her duty to her dead daughter finished. Everything she owned was fancy. "I like a little extra touch," was the way she put it. Her shopping hat had clusters of plastic grapes; the scarf around her neck was printed with gliding swans; her kitchen cabinets had glued-on felt donkeys; her sofa cushions, appliquéd poodles. "Get me my giraffe bag," she would say, and Virginia would come back holding a purse with a crocheted animal on its side. Or "my strawberry potholder." Or "my elephant sewing basket."

The beaded curtain that hung between the living room and dining room, and made a tinkling sound when one walked through, was like one she had seen in California. To one side of it were a pair of blue budgerigars in a cage, identical to birds she had seen in Florida.

Virginia was embarrassed by both place and people. Her grandfather (step) had a worthless son in Indiana in his thirties, and every night after the heavy meal he would lay down his fork, shift his huge stomach out of the way of the table edge, and complain, "I've got twenty-five thousand in that boy not counting high school. That's not including football uniforms. I tell him that to his face, the lot he cares." And then the grandmother would chime in about Virginia's two older sisters. "People are going to think they are not anything of any account at all. They'll have no reputation left when they get through. I gave them the best years of my life here in this house in this town full of folks with names you can't pronounce and wouldn't want them in your living room if you could. And that's the thanks I get. Living by themselves, and who knows what they do."

Nicholas found these conversations amazing. He was astonished to hear adults openly dissatisfied with their children. It seemed direct in a way he could hardly comprehend; and made him think again of Dr. Cavender.

He saw this as his future life: eating overcooked pot roast, listening to the garrulous in-laws, and touching Virginia at night.

22

Nicholas put an overcoat over his red sweater and went out of the train station into the cold. He drove his car the familiar route through the gray slushy snow across the river to the Kansas side of the city, up the bare hill (where he and Richard used to sled) to the imposing solitary house where his parents lived.

Home was all that he had expected. He smelled the revenge before he saw it. Fortunately—else he would have stepped on the smoldering stinking remains of a flayed and roasted dog. Scraps of singed hair lay in the snow. Nicholas stared at it, and could see—and understood that he was supposed to see—in the burnt tail and swollen charred face the cur that Richard had given him Thanksgiving.

An immolation for an engagement present.

Inside the library of the house his father was distraught and his mother swooned on the small couch. Richard, they explained, had happened upon a dreadful desecration on the sidewalk in front of their home. Had Nicholas seen it or had he been spared? They had called the city to come for it. Some dreadful prank.

In the hallway Richard was laughing silently. "Welcome home, brother," he said, as their father half-carried their mother upstairs. "You musn't try to give away what I give you."

2

At Home

Nell

———

"BUT I THOUGHT you and Tucker were so happy,"
Nell's sister Mo protested. "For Christ's sake, I wouldn't
have married his brother Trey if I didn't think we were all
one big happy family. The Woodard girls and the Drury
boys. You and Tucker. Me and Trey. Our little boys being
double first cousins. Us being more kin than kin—"

Nell's move out of her marriage and house had devastated
Mo, who thought that this time she had got herself a family
big enough and safe enough to stay put.

"I know," Nell said. "I'm sorry. Telling you is harder
than telling Tucker."

Mo could not answer for crying.

Mommy took the news even less well. "Leaving Tucker?
What do you mean, leaving? A trip? A separation? You're
in love? What are you saying?"

"I have asked for a divorce. He has said yes."

"Who is it, child? For God's sake why didn't you say
something sooner? Does Tucker know who it is?"

"It is nobody, Mother. I just don't want to be married to
Tucker."

"You don't move out on account of that. Something can
be worked out. You don't move out of a house; that was

Tucker's uncle's home. You have every right to it. You couldn't touch one like it these days for love nor money."

"Tucker and our son are going to stay in the house."

"Alfred? Your baby? You can't leave your baby! What will they think? They'll think that something sordid is going on. It's your dissatisfaction, LaNelle. They'll think there is another man and that Tucker won't let you go unless you leave his son behind. Is there? When someone twenty-five years old gets those circles around her eyes and that nervous way of pacing, I always know it's love. Is there, LaNelle? I will not be the last to know, hearing it in the grocery store by the artichokes, that LaNelle Woodard Drury has run off with her husband's friend."

The fear, of course, was not that there was someone else, but that there wasn't. Changing husbands in San Antonio when you could afford to was quite acceptable. Either you made your move when you could, when you saw that your husband had his eye on someone younger, thinner, richer, more interested and interesting than you; or you found in a new man what had been lacking in the old (breeding, or a bank). And everyone strained to see how far you moved up in the switch.

What was not acceptable was to leave because you were considering spending the rest of your life trying to catch the essence of the strange yellow haze filtered through the hardwoods on a hillside of blackberries in Kentucky, or distill the difference between the white of the coverlet in the Babies Room and the white of the Capodimonte roses. Spending one's life translating light was outside the framework of Mommy's world.

"Tucker didn't have a father himself," Nell told her mother. "He had to make do with an uncle. I'm not taking his son away."

28

Mommy's neck got tight as a turkey's. "It is not possible to abandon a child."

"I'm not giving Alfred away; I'm leaving him at home."

"What will you do?"

Nell looked far across the room, past it to other early times. "Paint, I think."

"I mean *do*—"

"If I'm careful there will be enough money."

"A Drury does not have to be careful, LaNelle."

"I am no longer a Drury, Mother."

"It's too much, LaNelle. Think of all the talk. They'll think there's someone else, no matter what you say . . ."

That was last week. This week Mommy had rallied. She had her speech down pat and had delivered it several times, in confidence, to friends: "I don't understand how they can be so different. I raised them both the same, they were my babies, as alike as twins, LaNelle and Moselle, people thought they were twins. Tommy couldn't tell them apart at the start. They even married brothers when they grew up, can you believe that, it was such a coincidence. And such good boys, raised without a father. I could sympathize with that, why if it hadn't been for Tommy, my own girls might have . . ." After a moment's pause: "But it seems if you have the artistic temperament then that will out. It's like a birthmark, someone said to me—wasn't that an intelligent thing to say?—it's like a birthmark and LaNelle has it and Moselle doesn't. It feels right to all of us for the boy to stay in the family; that's where he belongs. An artist is simply outside all that, you know."

To prove her point, she and Mo were taking Nell to a meeting of the Friends of the Bernais Museum of Fine Arts.

"Why are we dragging Nell to this bash, Mom? She'll

hate it. It's so boring. Nell, you'll wish you were watching 'The Price Is Right' on television. That's what the Friends do anyway, watch 'The Price—' "

"That will be enough, Moselle. I want to have this divorce out in the open. I do not wish to have people muttering about it behind my back, about my daughter who has left a Drury and her son besides. I want us to go and shake hands and face everyone and have it done with. LaNelle is an artist; this group supports artists. There is nothing they can do but welcome her."

"Yes, actually, Moms, there are several other things they can do," Mo said.

Mommy was prouder of being a Friend of the Bernais Museum of Fine Arts than of anything else in her life, even of her new house. The Friends spoke for Art, and therefore for Taste; rather, the Friends simply were taste, its personification. Mostly the group was so intermarried and crossbred that it was hard to identify anyone without mentioning a half dozen of the others. They had all gone to school with one another, made their debuts, been Duchesses, or Knights of the Order of the Alamo, been engaged to one another, married brothers (Mo and Nell were not the first), or sisters, or cousins, or even, if distant enough, their own cousins. The children had godparents, aunts, uncles, grandparents, playschools, and summer places all in common. To be a Friend was not to arrive, but to be already there.

Mo had got in because her husband was a Drury and their closest friends—who had been bridesmaids and groomsmen at one another's weddings—belonged. And if Mo was in, then, presumptively, she came from a proper family, and if she did then certainly her mother should have been there already. But that was all right; the Friends decided that Mommy after all had been a resident of Kentucky, the

Derby you know, when she was young, and pretended she had just moved into the neighborhood.

Nell had not thought to join.

She had never been to an evening with them, and was at a loss what to wear. "Oh, my, no, it's not dressy at all, not cocktail at all. This is really a meeting," Mommy had assured her. "Sort of an appreciation thing for the director. There'll be a lot of milling around to look at Terrence's paintings, some champagne, some speeches, and then we'll go home."

Nell had put on brown slacks and a brown shirt and gone to Mo's. "I don't have these tiny skirts they're wearing," she said. "Fix me up so I won't embarrass Mother."

Mo had produced a white satin scarf that she tied under the neck, and pulled the shirt out of the pants, somewhat like an artist's smock. She had lined Nell's eyes with something dark, and parted her hair in the middle. "You look famous," she declared. "Absolutely famous."

"Thanks."

"Darling, wonderful." Mommy had reached up and patted her eldest daughter's cheek. "You have such style. Subdued is just the right touch. Who could think ill of you, wearing that?"

"Actually, Moms, several people come to mind," Mo said.

They had gathered at Mommy and Tommy's new house. It was something that Mommy had waited eighteen years to get. It had been incredible luck, that lot, deep in the heart of the best part of town. It had never been on the market. It was the sloping back edge of a huge mansion on a hill, a triangular piece of ground between where the original lawns of the semi-palace had petered out by its carriage house, down on the road below, and its servants' quarters, adjacent to the carriage house. Both carriage house and servants' cottage had long ago been sold for six-figure sums, and transformed into two of the showplaces of the neighborhood, with gravel drives and careful planting beneath giant oaks and magnolias, and with the borders of white caladium that were in fashion.

Mommy had set her eye on the scrap of inaccessible land between them the week she moved to San Antonio, even as she put a down payment on the pink stucco with the pink flamingos. She had, in the course of careful time, made friends with the two families in the restored quarters. She had, even later, gained admission to the big Spanish palace on the hill that had once owned it all. It was eighteen years before they let the lot go, and that only after someone had climbed up the hill in the dark and tried to break into their electric fence. Who better, then, to sell it to but Mommy and Tommy? They would be guarddogs at the back gate.

For triple the money, Mommy had traded her pink house in to build another. This one was antique pink brick taken from a centuries-old mansion out in the country and carted into town. She had commissioned one of the resident artists at the Bernais to sculpt her a cluster of bronze flamingos to put in the garden by the reflecting pool, against a backdrop of pink caladium. Inside she had used faded pink handmade tile on the floors, and the result, with her bright yellow linen upholstering, looked, somehow, more French than Mexican. Her neighbors were enchanted, even envious, and took the credit for selecting her for that most difficult triangular lot between their homes.

Mo was pleased for Mommy, and for herself. It gave a standing, a stability, to her own family, so that she did not have to wholly rely on the Drury name. She made light of what the security represented to her, as was her way. "She's moved up to the cream of the cream, Nell, to Olmos Park.

32

Do you remember the aunts' help that we called Almost and Never? And it was forever before we learned their names were really Olmos and Neva? Well, I tell Moms she's olmos made it, now that she's in Almost Park. But she neva gets it."

Today they let Mommy show off the treasure she had ordered for her first Christmas party in the new house. It was the holiday special gift from Neiman-Marcus: an exact replica of the Parker Brothers' famous Monopoly, all made of candy. The board was bittersweet chocolate, and the money, properties, hotels, houses, dice, and chance cards were of pastel milk chocolate, buttercreams, and butterscotch. "Can you believe I did that? I just picked up the phone and ordered it. I thought I'd put it on the library table, just as if it were a real game, and see who spots it. It costs six hundred dollars but that's only half the cost of a week at the Greenhouse spa, and since I won't have time for that, well, I said to myself: You've earned it."

At the gathering of the Friends of the Bernais Art Museum they were met by Terrence DeMentil, their host, who wore a black tuxedo—except that the jacket was a cape lined with heavy ruby satin. "Ladies, charmed," he said, bowing low.

"Terry, dear, you know Moselle Drury, my daughter, and this is my other daughter, LaNelle Woodard Drury, who will be making her home in Santa Fe. She's the artist."

"Hello, Nell." He bowed slightly to let her know he knew who she actually was. "You've come as George Sand, I see, how clever. Most of the crowd refuses to honor my evenings by dressing."

"You are Count Dracula?"

"Of course. If you'll take my arm we'll precede these

33

ladies into the library. I have a small collection of purgatories, although I suppose a true connoisseur would call them dream pieces." He showed Nell three small drawings: a Hieronymous Bosch, a Gustav Doré, and a Max Ernst.

"Different, aren't they? The Bosch is reputed to be an early figure study for the Garden of Delights, a clear enough picture of everyone going to hell. The Doré, as you can see, is a frame from Dante's tour of hell; and the Ernst, my favorite, is an invention, a dream. That's what surrealism was, dreams on canvas. He uses two techniques, frottage and decalcomania, but you don't care about that, do you?"

"I don't. I know nothing of all this. My mother invents the idea of Artist to save face." She studied the sketches. "Everyone's hell seems so crowded."

"Wouldn't you imagine so?"

"I hadn't thought about it. I think I expected, you know, like Prometheus, hell being someplace you hung suspended for most of your life while they ate your liver out." She knew she sounded like an English major, but she had been.

"Did you just up and leave Tucker?"

"I left. I didn't up. I sort of exited sideways, I think."

"And the boy?"

"Are you going to tell me you were abandoned by your mother?"

"And now I wear a cape?" Terrence laughed. "No. I naturally just want to hear you tell about it. It's quite the buzz you know. It's been our major gossip for the week." He squeezed her arm warmly.

"Don't tell Mother. She's passing me off as news."

"Oh, we knew that. We could hardly wait to see her entrance. We knew you were coming."

"We?"

"The Friends. Come on. I'll introduce you. No one will say anything. Just look sly so they'll know that you know that they know and they'll think you darling."

Nell saw that the Art was not on the walls but in the dressing. The older women, Minnie's age, octogenarians, the really old ones, all wore long dresses, dark and beaded and made of chiffon with dark petticoats that didn't quite cover tan brassieres or large moles or dress shields of a not quite matching color. The women of sixty wore crêpe, draped to show off their diamonds. Those who had face lifts had Chinese eyes, and crêpey necks to match their gowns. They hugged and drank a lot, and Nell could see Mommy there in ten years or so. Mommy and her crowd wore designer dresses in Jacqueline Kennedy style: thick in the waist, narrow in the bosom, skirts above skinny knees. Those like Mo, young, all had on boots and short skirts lined with something that made them stand out like little girls'. There was no glimpse of breast or backend. Sex was not all right, she surmised, if all of you were kin.

Taking their cue from Terry, the Friends flocked around her, and gave her covert looks from across a shoulder, like ladies behind their church fans. The fact that Nell was as much as one of them, and had just packed up and walked out, was too titillating. They could try it out on themselves; could fling the threat at their mates. Could wish it on their enemies, or, sometimes, on their dearest Friends.

Nell had a good time. She said to Terry before they left, "How nice you were to prepare all this in advance. All I had to do was start to smile and then look away."

"You were a good study, dear. We'll do some little performance again soon. You might go with me to the Beaux Arts Ball. I'll be Prometheus if you like."

"And I'll be unbound." She laughed at knowing the expected response. It was comforting.

Mommy had had no champagne or cheese. "I simply don't take anything by mouth until dinner. It's that simple. I don't think about it, and then, at dinner, I think about it. That's how I keep my figure."

Nell came in for a visit at Mo's, where she had left her car. She wanted her sister to have time to digest the news of her leaving home.

The kitchen where they sat was huge and country. On a purple wall above brown floors and counters hung strings of red peppers, garlic cloves, a straw representation of a goose, a few ears of dried Indian corn.

"I like your wall," Nell said to Mo, not for the first time.

Mo studied the effect. "I'm thinking of adding a wire basket with onions. But they rot."

"Potatoes?"

"They rot, too." She poured them coffee. "There were some good lines this evening. Did you hear, 'If there was ever an impetus for apathy this collection is it'? Or 'My husband is a very private person, he doesn't even belong to Rotary'?"

Nell shook her head, smiling.

"There were these two fat women talking, elephants, and I heard one say, 'Oh, to be called birdlegs again.' "

Mo had changed into a loose dark dress the color of her D'Hannis tile floor, with Mexican embroidery around the neck. In the rich coffee browns and purples of the room she looked like a peasant woman, perhaps in Spain. She stalled a while with a tale from her volunteer work, about unwed mothers.

"We had twins who both made babies last week, Vonda Wandene and Rhonda Florene."

36

"You collect twins like Mother."

"The babies are named Up for Adoption. The same guy fathered both kids."

"Jesus."

"Maybe." Mo strained; she was not relaxed.

Nell asked after a moment, "Does it bother you, my leaving?"

"It takes some getting used to."

"It isn't something you get used to. Fathers have had this problem forever. Weekend visits, trips to the zoo. Weekend mother is not something we know what to do with. Think of me as the father. You wouldn't be bothered by that."

Mo said, "I'm not worried about Alfred. He's in the family. He owns half a bank already. When he's grown he'll have hotels on Park Place, and not chocolate ones. What I want to talk about is you."

Nell looked away.

"You get mad when Moms calls you an artist."

"I don't mind, it's her way."

"You think she's offering you an out."

"Herself an out."

"What I'm trying to say is that in her way Moms is right; you are an artist. You see everything that way."

"With a frame around it?"

"Don't be like that." Mo lost her big grin and twisted her curly hair. "You won't listen to me. No one listens to me when I am really trying to say something serious; they think I'm still being funny, and I'm really trying to say something."

Nell refilled her coffee cup and sat back down. "Sorry."

"Nell, you just aren't like other people. You aren't look-ing for what the rest of us look for, and that's what an artist is. I think that most people are interested in most people. What I mean is that I think most people do the same thing that most other people do. So they want to seem different. Look at me. Everyone has a red-tiled roof, so Mo has a blue-tiled one. Mommy plants pink caladium instead of white. I wouldn't have named my twins Frank and Stein, instead of Quatro and Cinco to go with Daddy Trey, if that hadn't already been the trend, if people hadn't been naming theirs things like Chase Manhattan and Merrill Lynch for years. I was letting them know we'd carried it too far. But I wasn't willing to do anything really different, like call them Tommy Jay and Billy Joe. Do you see?

"I notice, we all notice, the smallest change in each other, in hairdo or skirt length or shoe style or lipstick, and we say, 'Oh, you look fantastic,' to each other, 'That's so daring,' when we've made the teeniest bit of difference. But you aren't like that. You could live in a house with a red tile roof and have white caladium and name your kids for banks and you still wouldn't be us. Because you would see differences we don't see. You would see how none of us is really alike despite our wild efforts. I'm sometimes nervous with you, even I am, because I don't know what you're seeing really."

Nell looked at her sister. "You're saying that I make everyone anxious. I know that was true in my marriage. No matter what I did, it wasn't what he wanted. In bed—I couldn't get the hang of what he wanted. I used to lie in bed after he was asleep and wonder what other women did."

"Made more noise and lay stiller." Mo laughed.

"I should have asked." Nell laughed too.

"Do you know where this color scheme, the whole color scheme of this house, came from? I'll tell you. I'd still be doing pink and yellow like Moms if it weren't for you. You had on those brown slacks that you wear all the time, like now—I don't even notice them any more, maybe you have a dozen pair and alternate them, I used to think you were some kind of monk in school in all that brown—anyway, with a purple shirt you'd dug up, and Maudie Farmer, you don't know her, but she's the most 'in' person in San Antonio, sees you in the grocery and she says to me, 'Your sister always has such style.' And the next thing I know she comes to the Tea Room in a brown fringed skirt with a purple wool top and everyone freaks out because it looks so chic. I mean her daughter, Windsor, was three light years closer to being Fiesta Princess right then and there."

"You embellish."

"Okay. I invented Maudie. You wore that ugly shirt and pants until I decided I might as well live with it, paint my walls to match. Have it your way."

Nell walked around the kitchen. She wished Mo's little twins would wake from their nap. She did not like to talk about what she was doing. But Mo was her sister. She sat back down. "Actually, I am painting some."

Mo waited.

"But it is not what you think. When I was back in Kentucky visiting, the Christmas before I married Tucker, I tried to get the aunts' white china roses. I asked for them and Minnie said: 'Corpse still warm and they're cutting it up.' Something to that effect. So I let it go. Now Vinnie's gone, and I'm sure Minnie will give the roses to the Louisville cousins. It doesn't matter. I have painted them for my room. And I've done a picture of a bowl of eggs. Hardboiled ones like the ones I put in the Babies Room the Easter we left."

"Which I mushed." Mo giggled.

39

"Well, the picture recalls them to me. It's hard to talk about. You mustn't think I'm holding back on you."

"Will you try it for real? Will you go to Santa Fe like Moms tells everyone you are? A lot of artists from here go there, it's the light or the atmosphere or something. Will you try?"

Nell studied her cup. "I think Santa Fe is for Maudie Farmer."

"Just try it, Nell . . ."

"Tucker could handle it better if I were a failed painter in another state." She considered her sister. "Why does it matter so much to you?"

"Because—" Mo wiped the sweat off her hands "—because it's what I'd most love to do in the whole world."

Nell had no real desire to leave what she had freshly made in her new gray shingled half-house: a well-constructed order. She had at last her own White Room, with her Eggs and Roses. She had the time of day when she worked, and the time when she let it rest.

In the early mornings she walked down the hill from her small half a house, past the big houses, down through the streets to the old smaller ones with bigger trees. A trio of neighborhood dogs had begun to follow her to the edge of the residential area. She called them Fred (a basset), Red (a setter) and Ted (some sort of woolly pup)— Mommy's rhyming seemed to sit quite sweetly on a pack of dogs—and when a fourth had joined them, a ragged, pregnant bitch, she christened her Shred.

She had breakfast at a small shop on Broadway with all the teachers and office workers and fathers with overnight custody—fried eggs, biscuits, lots of coffee—while the dogs waited for her at the last yard. By the time they started back the convent school was full of children, and the daddies from the big houses were leaving for work.

At home she climbed the outside stairs to the room where the messy thick dress she was trying to translate onto canvas lay spread all over the floor.

Except if it were Alfred's day to come; then she waited in the living room, which was small and also her bedroom. It had her white bed, with brass head and foot, set against the wall like a couch, still empty of the china baby dolls she needed to make it a Babies Room. Above the bed, to one side, was the replica of the White Eggs. And over the old black marble fireplace was her portrait of the Capodimonte roses. She had no rugs for the dark wood floors; and only one brown chair for company, her son.

"Hello, Mother," he would say as he stood outside her door, his other grandmother waiting in the purring Oldsmobile to make sure he was received. "May I come in?"

"Hello, Alfred."

She wanted to give her son what she had wanted from her father and not got. She wished her daddy had stayed in Mineral Springs, in another part of town, maybe a not-nice part of town, and that she had been allowed to go see him and meet his woman (whom she always pictured looking like Belle Watling in *Gone With the Wind*). He would be laughing and drinking whiskey and he would take her on his knee and ride-a-cock-horse. And then she could have seen why he had to leave Mommy and her girls, why he could not stand it. She had wanted that fiercely, a glimpse of an alternate world. Even if he had sold insurance and married a plump woman who liked to bake from mixes and covered their bed with a chenille spread, that would have been all right. She could understand that. You just wanted to know what was worth leaving for.

She could offer that to Alfred: another way of doing. Daddies could do that. Mothers could not; they had to live with you. Mothers never took their eyes off you and they didn't take you too seriously. You asked mothers, "How do I know I'm not dreaming?" and they said, "Pinch yourself, honey, and if it hurts you're awake." Or they said, "The pokey way you're moving around here today I'm not sure myself." But daddies would look up from their papers, or have you down to spend the night, and say: "I never figured that out myself."

The whole time she had been Alfred's parent they had had a sort of civil formality with one another anyway.

"Hello, Alfred," she had greeted him in the hospital, having given birth to him six hours before. She had tried to imagine Tucker as such an infant in the arms of that hovering person who was his mother, or herself smothered against Mommy Estelle. Each with some faded photo-album daddy looking over her shoulder.

She had opened her bed jacket to nurse and found it awkward for them both. Alfred did not know what to do and she didn't either. She had assumed that the baby came equipped with knowledge of such things, and that the mother had only to pay attention, to take heed, and follow the baby's cues. But Alfred, reserved, thoughtful, waited for instruction. For half an hour she fumbled with her breast and his mouth. Finally they gave him a bottle in the nursery and the next time he took her nipple firmly, as a substitute, gamely working harder for the same thing, not quite sure it was worth the effort.

She had not known how to raise her son in the accepted way. "I don't know what I should think about that," her attitude said, "or how to deal with it fairly." Or, "I'd really rather not have to punish you if we could avoid it." And

42

he, the small son, on his part, conveyed, "I'd as soon not misbehave because I don't know what the results will be and it will make trouble and I don't feel that I know how to handle that." So he was a "good boy" and she hadn't meant for that to happen, but at least she did not reward him for it, but treated it as a sort of cowardice on both their parts. "I'm sorry," she implied, "that you have to be good because I haven't sorted out what I should do if you're not." And he, in his turn, did not have to feel guilty because he was not a troublemaker the way parents liked boys to be so that they could act things out themselves.

When they were alone they had never talked much. "How does this work?" he might ask, diffidently, checking to see if she was occupied and if it was all right to disturb her. "I think like this," and she would show him and let him know that it was fine to ask.

Their weekly visits had the same cordial air.

"I'm going to paint this afternoon," she said on one of the first times. "Did you bring something to do?"

"Dad said—I was gonna bring my Lego, but Dad said—"

"What?"

"You'd have something for me to do."

"At my house you have to find it. We'll go get a hamburger and then we can pick up something for you to keep here. Crayons or something."

"Can I get comics?"

"Can you read them?"

The four-year-old answered firmly, "Kind of."

"Then you can keep a stack here." (She hoped they were forbidden at his father's house.)

But mostly Alfred played in the back yard with the visiting dogs, who flopped down panting after their walks, or played with the tire swing she had put up on the huge

43

shedding pecan tree beside the yellowed weedy patch of ground where once a garage had been. That was something that she could do for Alfred: take her eyes off him. That's what daddies did.

There was the fear that he would be kidnapped, abducted, hit by a crazy driver from the street, bitten by a rabid dog, while she worked. And then she would have to say, "Well, Tucker, you see, I was painting and I left him outside," and bear the full consequences of her irresponsibility. But she had made that choice.

Things were amicable when he left. "I'm glad you came, Alfred."

"Okay," he said, as he politely let himself out the door to the waiting car of his other grandmother.

Upstairs where she worked was an east room looking down on the yellowed patch of weeds. Its floor was gray linoleum, made like some sort of giant wobbly pebble. She loved the room.

She was trying to learn to paint. She knew nothing. She had a book, ten books—and charts of all the colors that went into making white, the blues and yellows and grays and pinks of white. Painting had not been how she thought it would be. She had bought canvases and talked to art stores and got her books and come home and gone up the outside stairs. And then: nothing told you how it really worked.

There were pages on line and light and shadow and shape, but nobody said to you how you got the picture in your head out through your fingers onto the canvas. It was a matter of having what you were seeing in you become apparent as the same thing outside you. Between recollecting and reproducing there was a missing step.

44

She had started to paint the roses from her clear memory of them. Then, when that did not work, she had bought a dozen white ones from the florist and arranged them on the table. And then, when that did not work, she had written to Minnie for a snapshot—but only a rest home replied.

Finally, she had picked up a San Antonio flower book called *Gardening in South Texas*, and there was what she needed. The illustrations looked like facsimiles of photographs, not once or twice but three times removed from the real roses. She had selected the Peace Rose to be the aunts' Capodimonte. It was the same velvety contoured glazed sort of rose. The illustration was in flat black and white, light and dark in easily understandable ways that Nell could replicate with her slick acrylics. And she had: put onto canvas a remembrance of the white china roses on the mantle in the Rose Room.

It had gone the same way with the eggs. She had posed a dozen real eggs, two dozen times, and two dozen more. And there was no way that the eggs on the table could transfer Egg onto canvas. Finally she went to the Seed 'n' Feed store and got a booklet on laying hens; and there found a page of black and white illustrations of the best of Rhode Island Reds. And that reproduced bunch of curves that looked like eggs but weren't eggs was something she could imitate.

(She learned that the white of the eggs had more yellow on the dark parts than the white of the roses, which had more gray.)

Now she was constructing on the floor a model of a wedding dress to copy onto canvas. She wanted to build the folds and puckers and gathers and scattered beads into the

45

weight and motion of a real dress. She had started with cutouts, wanting something two dimensional rising slightly into three. An imitation of real, the way a cookie figure that is an imitation of a human becomes a thing in itself, a Gingerbread Man, with its raisin buttons and citron eyes.

What she was doing now was learning to construct a copy of what she saw clearly in her mind. She could not depend on catalogues and garden books forever. She had to learn to make her own; you could not paint without a model. Light was too dazzling and shadow too elusive to look upon directly.

What this meant was the following: she would build bit by bit the shape and outline and feel of the Dress before her on the floor, and then she would give that to the hands to translate. The rest was up to them; to learn, by guess or feel or memory, or most of all by trial and error, to show the Dress itself.

She built a skirt of tissue paper, with paper doilies for adornment, gauze for a bodice, rice for seed pearls, and white flour and glaze of sugar for texture and shine. She made it larger than life-size, with folds and puffs and tender tucks and nipped-in waist. It was, she saw (or perceived that she had already seen), a Wedding Dress. Not her own, but such a dress as that in the dreams of a small girl playing paper dolls in a White Room.

It wasn't good.

That went without saying. What was the surprise was how very much she cared that the dress did not look as it did in her head. Instead, as she began to paint its likeness onto canvas it took on a whitewashed, thick, stiff, heavy appearance. It was only, still, a gross approximation. She had not reckoned with how terribly much it mattered to her

46

that what her mind saw and her eyes copied her hands could not translate.

What she had in no way counted on was the length of time that it would take to do it right.

In the end it was not Mo or Mommy who forced the decision. It was Terrence and his little hells. It was the elegant old patrons of the arts in their yellowed dentures.

The point was that if the Friends wanted Art, they acquired it. There was no place in their world for amateur, or apprentice. No place in their appreciation for spending a dozen years, or two, to paint an image that could be purchased in an afternoon. In a half dozen years the Friends would say: "What are you doing these days, Nell, dear?" and she would tell them that she had at last made one white dress that worked. And they would look tactfully over their shoulders at kissing cousins, and clear their stringy throats.

If she were off in Santa Fe, the Friends could think of her as one of them: indulging an interest, standing at an easel before the purple mountains. Sending postcards home. They would not be confronted with the time it took, or solitude it cost, to learn to show what you already saw. In Santa Fe no one would see the one hundred failed canvases heaped outside the back door in the scornful sun.

Daddies, she told herself, did that; they went away and came back for visits. You flew out to see them. She could do that.

She could go away from home.

"I thought we were happy," Tucker had said when she left him. That puzzled part-owner of a bank.

"Why?"

"Because nothing was wrong."

"I thought we weren't, because nothing was right."

It all depended on where you stood.

Nick

———◆———

NICHOLAS HAD LOOKED forward all week to driving to his parents' on Sunday. He was ashamed of his anticipation. As eagerly as he had meant to leave it behind, he now wanted to return to that dark house of his parents. It was the order he wanted back, and meals that were served, and conversation after coffee.

His brother he could do without, but Virginia would not come unless Richard was to be there also, as she detested his parents. "They think you married trash and never let me forget it. I think if you stuck a pin in either of them they'd pop like a balloon with their own hot air. Richard is the only human at that mausoleum."

On the drive from Topeka past black farms and grain elevators, he felt homesick for the sight of Kansas City's smokestacks, and railyards, and the river, and sledding hill. He and Virginia did not come often. Mother's Day was a command performance; they left the little girls at home.

In church he read the implacable Calvanist doctrine of the saved and the damned: "Some men and angels are predestinated unto everlasting life and others foreordained to everlasting death . . . and their number is so certain and definite that it cannot be either increased or diminished."

This had been the message of his childhood.

He had spent the years of his adult life, he supposed, try-ing to disprove it.

More and more he was coming around to thinking that Lamarck had been right in his insistence on the transmission of acquired characteristics. If imprints of chemical changes could be carried into the germ plasm, as seemed possible, and if natural selection could favor those individuals whose genetic makeup would go along with chemical changes, then chemical changes could be handed down as genetic changes. It might be that dozens of different genes would act together in a new way for one change; each gene having previously had quite different expressions in other parts of the body. This would be true if the genes determined re-lation as well as content; for if the relation changed, so would the effect of the gene.

He had not gone into genetics for the same reason he had not gone into psychiatry. Because at the time he began his graduate studies both of these fields presented a view of the world as foreordained as the doctrine of Presbyterian predestination. The genetic code seemed (was), according to Darwin, a closed system since the start of time; and, for Freud, our forgotten past acted as sole determinant of our future.

His subsequent studies with the brain had shown that the chemistry of the mother's brain at the time of delivery af-fected the infant from the start. Therefore, you had but to change her chemistry, and you changed the future. Nicholas needed that conviction: that in whatever system you chose to work, the result was not predetermined.

As they had always done, Nicholas and his brother stood diametrically opposed on their view of the world. Where Nicholas wanted to prove that progress was possible, Richard sought to set his part of Kansas back five hundred years.

Both brothers had begun in biochemistry, but Richard's interest had gone far afield, as he liked to say. Immediately out of graduate school, he had sold all of his personal stock and annuities and bought eight thousand acres of what had once been part of a vast two hundred thousand acre tract called the Tallgrass Prairie, where buffalo had grazed, and on which Richard intended to restore in the most minute detail the original plains.

"I'm going to turn the world around," he had proclaimed to his parents as they protested the liquidation of funds that were never mentioned, and that were to exist as set up in perpetuity. "I'm not going to be here in perpetuity," Richard had told them, "and the only thing the Clarks have done so far in perpetuity is be innocuous and unknown. I'm going to put my name in the history books. Luther Burbank got all that glory for a walnut or two and a gladiolus bulb, didn't he? And our own famous Kansas Aggie David Fairchild went off to Washington and set up an Office of Cereal Investigation. They had all the breaks, but they thought small. Burbank read Darwin's *The Variation of Animals and Plants Under Domestication*, and went into labor pains with the Shasta daisy. Fairchild did him one better, and had Alfred Russel Wallace to dinner, the man who developed his theory of natural selection one nocturnal emission before Darwin did, and what did Fairchild do with all that smart? Taught us how to process a better macaroni. I'm thinking big. I'm going to show the world that it can restore its lands to where they were before man macadamized them; I'm going to be the one they remember as turning this downhill slide around."

"Fairchild married Alexander Graham Bell's daughter, that's how he did that," Virginia told Nicholas, having looked the name up in the encyclopedia. "That's how he could afford to cruise around the world looking at palm trees or whatever. But you tell me how your brother can sit up there owning most of the state and letting it all go to seed, and pay for that, and for all those legal battles he has with the U.S. Congress to keep them from making it into a national park. You tell me how come he can afford to be up to his ass in his precious grass, and we're living so crowded in this house it's like a tenement?"

Nicholas reluctantly had explained about annuities, and the matter had come up at least once a month for the first year or two.

"You mean to tell me your folks have that kind of money—?"

"They don't. This was in trust." But he did not like to talk of it. He wanted to pay his own way with his research job at the university, and he wanted that to be enough for this woman who was his wife.

But it was to be expected that Richard made trouble for Nicholas no matter what he did. No doubt he was wiring his grasslands as he once had his rose bushes, so that no intruder could take a leak.

His brother, having skipped the church service, awaited them on the doorstep of the big narrow house. He had with him a new girlfriend, Cynthia, a forest ranger who (he reported out of hearing of their parents) conducted her watch for forest fires stark naked. She had gone to work for the Park Service out of college, done her time cleaning latrines at Yellowstone, and had decided that rangers had all the fun. She was the newest fan of Richard's prairie project.

"This is my brother, Nick," Richard said, introducing

him to Cynthia. "He's an envious son-of-a-bitch, my brother. When I was a kid I wired up some rose bushes to keep Wat Tyler the First on his toes, and Nick here admired the idea so much that now he makes his living, or should anyway, one of these days, shocking the sense out of white rats. And this—" he turned to Nicholas' wife "—is Virginia. She runs in the family."

The young woman, who looked tan, sturdy, and wore her blond hair in a thick braid, held out her hand. Virginia took it reluctantly.

Despite the Mother's Day meal of lamb and new peas and lemon cake, the strain of his mother holding court in the library afterwards affected Nicholas as it always did.

In fact, if anything, he found himself more vulnerable to her than he had been before. This had to do with his relationship with Virginia, he thought. At the beginning his wife had seemed so quick to get right to the end of things; now he saw that it was because she had no patience with their middle. That which was complex angered, frustrated, and, finally, defeated her. So it had come about that it was now Nicholas who moved slowly and circumlocutiously toward resolution. Lately he had begun to fear that he was becoming like his mother; that it would be he who never got back to the mahogany table.

Mary Ann smoothed her silken skirt and waited for her cue.

"Your mother has special news for you today," their father said. He looked at his wife proudly. "She has written an article for the *Reader's Digest*." He waited expectantly for her to pick up the tale.

"I called it 'How it Feels to be a Russian in America Today,'" she told them, folding her hands together in a gesture of composure. "It was, you see, I wanted to let people know, this land was formed by the landed gentry of many, including . . . naturally, of course there were peasants, too, immigrants, one can't discount . . . my own country, Russia, that is, hers, those nobles who fled terror in their own lands, they of all the peoples here could most understand the dangers of the terrors still being inflicted overseas, the danger of the terrorism that might be visited on America, they were in this way the most loyal of all Americans. My father's wife," she continued earnestly, "who wasn't actually my mother, although I didn't know this growing up you see, and certainly you would not have either, gentle people trying to spare their child, the same thing I would have done I'm sure, but we who are from another sort of plains, who had fled, that is, I'm sure that was the reason that she, my father's wife, White Russians to be sure, not the other kind. I more than any mother, if I had small children today, would make public what we had, would not allow tyranny . . . I said in that article, as you can read . . . The most incredible thing, to think such a magazine, such a respected, if no doubt middle or even working class, although those vocabulary tests can't be designed, still . . . for them to call and make such a fuss, with her children, my brothers . . . You can see the spot I'm in, I'm sure, when my intent was to make the point that no one could be more patriotic than . . ."

Their father supplied the necessary exposition. Mary Ann had written an article that had been accepted, and for which she had received, but not cashed, a check for five hundred dollars. What had made trouble was the *Digest*'s policy of calling everyone whose name was mentioned in the article to read them the lines about themselves. It seemed that

54

all concerned—Mary Ann's stepmother, and stepbrothers —had been unwilling to have their names included. Frank did not dwell on that, but passed on to the policy behind the calls. "To be sure this is to prevent lawsuits. After all, what is to prevent someone with less integrity than your mother from making up out of whole cloth stories that have no basis in fact? You cannot blame them. On the other hand, your mother was not advised of the policy at the start, or even upon acceptance of her article, and I'm sure had she been she would have preferred not to submit herself to such an ordeal."

Mary Ann threaded her fingers together. "But I should think they would be, what is there to hide, if we were at war with Great Britain again and there were lords or earls here in exile, we would surely, in a land where tyranny . . . I should think they would be, she would be, proud to acknowledge . . ."

Their father soothed her. "These are times when everyone appears scared of his shadow, dear heart. I thought your article very brave. We are all most proud of you, your sons and I."

Nicholas could not think of words to say, as his mind moved slowly both over the information given and that which was somehow withheld.

Richard did not hesitate but moved right in with a new scheme to get publicity for his grasslands. "I'm going to invite Lyndon Johnson to come stand in the fields in his cowboy boots. Remember the spread he got back with that camel driver he brought over from Pakistan? The one who was all over three pages of *Life* magazine giving the finger in Urdu? Picture the President claiming the tallgrass, astride a buffalo."

55

Their parents did not respond. Frank found little to relate to about his sons' work, lacking sympathy with both mail-order rats and out-of-print grass. Neither seemed engaged in the scholarship he had intended for them.

Mary Ann told Cynthia and Virginia a winding tale about her mother, who was not really her mother, and a pond that they had had at their house, which was really not their house but a summer place they sometimes used.

In the driveway, departing, Richard asked his brother, "What did you think of our Russian mother today?"

Nicholas hesitated. "Could she have written it?" He could not put it together. If his mother could write an essay with a start and finish, why couldn't she talk that way? Was it a function of having to put it down in orderly sentences? Or was it that the brain itself proceeded in a line but that the words could not come out that way due to anxiety? He felt if he could read the article, he could tell from that. If it was different from her speech, then there were conclusions in that brain somewhere.

"Never mind the literacy question," Richard said. "The point is *why?* I don't get it. Why the public announcement of her pseudo-citizenship all of a sudden? And in print. It's like Dad had suddenly dropped the news that he'd sold an account of his not making good at Harvard to *Argosy* magazine. It is not possible in a family that thinks you only get written up once, when you die, provided you die in a respectable manner. Every time I show them a feature story on my plot of Mead's milkweed or ten-mile stretch of Indian grass they purse their proper lips in horror. This has to take the cake for total unexpected act of the decade."

"I thought your mother was sort of sweet," Cynthia said,

not sure what was going on.

"She's a certifiable loon," Virginia said.

"You wanted in this family, don't forget," Richard reminded his brother's wife.

"To answer your question," Virginia said to Nicholas in the car on the way home, "You know your dad wrote it. I can hear it now: 'Dear, just dictate it to me, let your little mind relax and I'll take it down for you. Don't mess your dainty hands with an old fountain pen.' "

Nicholas flinched.

"Don't take it so hard."

He didn't answer.

"Maybe he'll start writing her monologues. That would be an improvement."

"He said she wrote it."

"You always want a happy ending like in the movies: she gets out of her wheelchair in the last frame and runs toward his plane and her legs aren't crippled any more. It makes it hard as shit on us who have to work without miracles."

Virginia had accused him of wanting easy resolutions before. It was not true. She was the one who wanted solutions that required no effort on her part. His mother was evidence enough that he had been raised unraveling tangles. It carried over into his work: in the lab he could spend four months testing brain analyses only to find that nothing had been learned; or set the tedious electrode implants and then have a rat disconnect the leads, or die for no apparent reason. And start over.

His wife, he considered, not for the first time, would have done better with Richard. They had an affinity—or he projected that they did. He was unable, in honest moments, to decide if that were true, or if it was his unacknowledged wish to give Virginia back to his brother.

Walking into his own house assaulted him as always. He could not reconcile himself to being in this place where he apparently lived. It was always as if he were there temporarily, trying not to convey his distaste, making every effort to disassociate himself in order for it to be possible for him to stay. He had never known that such things could happen to houses. The dirty sinks, crusted commodes, stale odors, mildewed clothes, grapefruit rinds. The room you entered when you came into the house, the supposed living room, had diapers, toys, a pallet for sleeping, food days old and dried to the couch and the floor, clothes dropped on the rug and chairs, papers, cigarettes, kitty litter. Every room downstairs and up, although he seldom went up, was the same. Every room smelled of urine and food.

He had got a cleaning woman for Virginia. Had learned to wash the dishes and disinfect the bathroom. But these efforts were so small, so meager in the onrush of disorder that two people, and then four people, had made of their life.

He could not live with it forever. Something in his body had begun to crawl away where it could not be reached. He had tried to tell her. Had tried to tackle the house himself. Sisyphus pushing the stone uphill; Hercules sweeping out the mythological stable. Her retort was that women could not do all they were expected to. It was too much for anyone.

He did not know how to counter that. It did not seem the issue, but he could not argue it.

"You want it all," Virginia accused. "The grand dame in

the library holding forth on Sartre, the maid in the kitchen, the British nanny in the nursery, and then, ah, here's the rub, you still want what you've got in the bedroom."

His small daughters, Joey and Johnnie, named for Virginia's older sisters, were still awake. He and she had decided, as her style of childrearing distracted and upset his mother, to get a sitter on such occasions as Mother's Day. "Which are the only times we go to Kansas City. In other words, you'd just as soon your folks never saw them, isn't that it?"

He hugged his little girls, aged one and two. Both so dark and musky and round and foreign to him. His daughters and his wife were a unit who knew rules that he did not, spoke a language that he did not, giggled and cried and stormed and talked to each other with and without words in tones and for reasons that he had no inkling of or part in. It was a closed shop.

Virginia found him in the bedroom. A beaded curtain separated the dressing area from the bed. Lavender flowers splashed the sheets and spread. A big wicker basket of dried cattails sat by the window. One orange bulb was over the bed. (The gold glow, Virginia said, made her skin pink, whereas a pink light made it sallow.)

Nicholas had made the room straight except for a pile of clothes in one corner, and the grapefruit rinds left under the bed from Virginia's insomniac eating. He wanted to make love. There were a few hours before the little girls piled on their parents' bed with boxes of sticky dry cereal, and before Virginia rose up—angry at motherhood, the house, her life, at the fact that there was no one like her grandmother to comb the snarls out of her hair.

"She was prettier than I, wasn't she?" Virginia was in a gown that showed her breasts and hid her heavy legs. Her white arms had put on weight with her pregnancies and dimpled slightly. "He always brings around prettier girls to let me know he did better than me."

Nicholas did not want to talk about his brother. He wanted only to make love; to feel her body and have that be all right, to have a truce, and go to sleep. He answered carefully, "Cynthia? I thought she looked like a prairie girl. That's fitting, wouldn't you say? I don't think Richard is out to drag in pretty girls as such. I think he brings whoever is around. You remember we had Carol the botanist all winter?" Nicholas had moved over toward his wife and was caressing her. "The only beauty he ever brought to our house was you."

"How do I know you don't look each one over wanting to make a trade?"

"Look at the behavior."

"Oh, goddam it, don't talk to me like a lab assistant. I don't know what goes on in your head. I know you want to stick it in, but I don't know what you're thinking. Maybe you want it because Cynthia—you always say their names back to me so that I can't forget them—got you hot. That blond hair."

"I want you, Virginia. That's why I'm here." He touched her and tried to soothe her into lying beside him.

"He flaunts those girls who still have their figures. It's so he can say he didn't want me after all. He never lets me forget he dumped me."

"Why can't you think that I took you instead?"

"Because it isn't something you would have done in a million years if he had wanted to marry me." She leaned down over him and shouted. "The dog. What did you do about the dog?"

Nicholas got out of bed and went into the bathroom.

Did she bring the dog up every time they saw Richard? He thought she did. He thought she did that to make him jealous, to show, at the least, that Richard was not unaffected by her going.

The dog would not go away. It rose up in him sometimes, the stench and swollen sight, and would not go away. His enmity toward his brother, begun at the gold birthday party, had hardened forever with the dog.

When he got back from the bathroom she was out of her gown, with it pulled up between her legs. "I'm sorry about the dog. I wish to God you'd never told me."

"Let's forget it."

"Do you really want me?"

He began to show her. He was back to their honeymoon and being allowed all over again access and entry, back to the small noises and panting that she thought to be sexy, and the slight moans that she made if he touched her anywhere, and the way she sometimes opened her eyes quickly to be sure he was transported by her. He touched, a ritual, the four corners of her breasts, imagining the ladies of the night under the streets of London. He touched the aquamarine wings of the butterfly pricked into the flesh of her shoulder. And for a time, it was all right.

3

Santa Fe

Nell

———◆———

"GET THIS." They were all sitting around a table in the courtyard at the Blue Parrott, reading. "Dallas has a magazine called *Acquire*."

"Dallas is a city called Acquire."

"For collectors."

"Who isn't?"

"Let's start one of our own. Accuse?"

"Accede?"

"Askance?"

"Here's looking at you, Askance."

Nell was in a pink blouse and brown pants. She had given in to Santa Fe, where everything was washed in red. The shadows at the Parrott were lavender. The white cloth on their table, beneath great hanging baskets of bougainvillea, was pink. The green leaves, washed with the same slanting sun, were copper. All greens were brown; all yellows, orange; all blues, purple. All paintings—the fabulous mammoth Scholder Indians—were in the only possible colors: purple, brown, pink, orange.

Nell was at a table with so-called artists, most amateur, none very good. The women at the table were in love with men (men gone to other places or in their past.) The men were also. Nell had been going around with a homosexual who did not want to be presented that way, so he took Nell out and sometimes stayed overnight so that they could wander in late and lazy on a Sunday morning in their pants and pink shirts to have gin and orange juice and blueberry waffles and strawberry pancakes and talk of art and painting. He would stroke her knee and be knowledgeable about her work and her bedroom. It didn't matter. Everyone knew. As long as you didn't admit to it.

It didn't matter: that was how it was in Santa Fe. You drank and ate and rode out into the mountain edges on horseback, or you met at the café they had decided they liked best that week. La Posada had got crowded with tourists, people in print shirts and hats against the ceaseless sun. People who thought it all mattered and asked for blue corn tortillas or where was the Cathedral of the Archbishop. They, the crowd, moved on out the river road to the Parrott. Now someone had said this morning that it was time to try the new place, My Adobe Hacienda, which some piano player from Jersey had opened so he would have a place to pretend he was Hoagy Carmichael. That on Sunday mornings he fixed whatever he felt like having that Sunday, which was all you could get, and it might be cheese soup cooked in a pumpkin or squash turnover with maple syrup, but the singing was strangely good and you all sat around on stools at an oblong bar that faced not bottles but pots of geraniums and caged birds. They decided they would try it: this place, the Parrott, was getting known and noisy. You didn't know the people who came in any more.

"We could have a column called 'How Bizarre is too bizarre?' "

"B-a-z-a-a-r?"

"Yes, a shopping column."

"How about a gossip column: 'Let's Name Drop.' "

They were high on gin and strawberries and syrup and pastries that Sunday morning. The men wore tight pants. The women loose tops. Both groups showed a little, but just for the mood, not expecting anything to come from it.

The magazine game continued. Someone suggested an advice column entitled, "What Do You Mean, Too Young?" Another, "What Do You Mean, Too Old?"

They lapsed in the lavender light into an old game, a favorite. In which they spoke to one another in overheard lines from other parties. This wasn't as much fun as when someone new was in the group; then the outsider stared from one to the other of them, wondering what was going on, trying to make sense of the desultory conversation that everyone seemed to follow without any trouble.

"These are hard times for the First Amendment," Woody, Nell's date, said, stretching his long legs in their sleek pants, slitting his eyes slightly to signal the game. He was having anisette instead of gin, because he had read of it and liked to order it. He hated the taste, but that more or less summed up Santa Fe.

"Art has cultural redolence," came from across the table.

"Perhaps we should all sit around remembering Proust."

"The retarded color beautifully."

The group had gathered Nell into their midst after her first show. She had been coaxed by Luciana, an older woman who owned a gallery, to hang the best of her Dresses in a late midsummer exhibition.

They had all come to see Luciana's protégé, and sip champagne, and look about for famous names.

Nell thought the show a meager lot for almost six years'

work. Only in the last six months had she been able to make the canvas show what she saw. There was a second Wedding Dress, two versions of a pinkened Christening Dress (one tiered and crumbling as if it had been packed away a hundred years). Three white Convent Dresses, identical as paper dolls. Not many more.

It had not been her, Nell, the group had seized upon at the show, but its extravagant review; they needed one token Artist in their midst to lend their assemblage credibility:

> *Immense garments in acrylics on canvas which suggest the emotional reticence of Manet . . . Although it is influenced by his redefinition of painting as "picture of pictures," and absorbed by a similar preoccupation with light, one can see in Miss Woodard's disciplined portraiture a distinctly original expression.*

"You'll be our original, darling," they said, flocking about her. If they could not have a big name, then they would take a new face.

After that, someone would call to tell her when they were all getting together. And she would go. It felt good, because the crowd was pink and orange and purple and easy and fit in with the surroundings. She could not imagine coming to the Blue Parrott alone. There would have been no reason to be there. She liked moving en masse. It was new to her. It gave her a sort of invisibility she had always wanted—back in the days of her brown coat and brown shoes and brown skirt—and had not known how to achieve. But this was better, as you appeared never to be alone, were never singled out, but were one of the group. She had written Terry DeMentil that he would be welcome to come join the Friends of the Blue Parrott.

At night they went to one of their studio homes to talk of Art. Not what Nell was preoccupied with, the red wash, what shade of carmine or alizarin crimson or cadmium deep red or purple madder or magenta (depending on the angle of the sun) covered everything; but who was doing a show, who he was living with, the food or horses he might raise, where he went to get out of the balling red sun, whether he had been recently to Spain, whether he had been to other deserts besides Santa Fe, and, primarily, whether his things were overpriced and too obvious or underpriced and too obvious. All of that was good for Nell. Safe and interesting and not relevant to what she did in the red mornings or purple evenings with her giant baby pink Christening Dress, which loomed over her from morning to night.

They sometimes talked of places: the light in the interior of El Santuario de Chimayo on the purple bleeding Jesus, a certain *penitente morada* discovered in the mountains, a small adobe house, whose owner was unidentified, where someone had gone away to be alone and consider painting. Or it might be some ancient ruined pueblo whose tenebrous interior required a reworking of all one's previous pictures, perhaps a black wash on the canvas; and a rethinking of the vision Art provided, maybe a decision to paint only at night, in the dark. These evenings at someone's studio could be left at any time; the dialogues were ongoing, resumed at a later date, interrupted and picked back up, there were no hard feelings. If you left or if you stayed: it didn't matter.

As long as you didn't make pottery or rugs.

When it was Nell's turn to have the crowd over, she had gazpacho, and a chili that she made with hominy, and Texas beer, and gin, and anisette for Woody. She had taken a roll of film of a small stucco church up in the mountains above

69

Taos, in a village without a true name where the red was somehow blocked in the morning light by shadows from forests on higher slopes; it was a handful of photographs to work from that had flat blue skies, blue plaster altars, white crosses in the courtyard, and grayed shadows on the whitewashed chapel. They admired the snapshots and talked of such villages and the benefit of getting off somewhere to paint. They were impressed with her for having found a place so out of the way that it was not yet even an Out of the Way Place. That reinforced the view that she was different. "You're our original," they said.

Her curved eggs, papery roses, and flattened Wedding Dress were taken as her props, not to be observed too closely—as theirs were birdcages with pierced silver birds, or dozens of baskets suspended from the ceiling, or masses of paper flowers. It didn't matter. The thing was to be casual and say: Come on by, it's my turn, bring someone if you like, wear whatever you want. That was the thing to say in Santa Fe.

Woody, now, was pressing a hand on her linen leg and that usually meant he was needing to be taken for her date.

She leaned forward until her dark hair brushed his cheek, and whispered to him a few words. He squeezed her shoulder. His eyes were on the beautiful young man with the deep tan and crumpled ear who was with Luciana, the gallery owner.

The group had moved into another of its games. The origin of this one was before Nell's day; it seemed something that had been passed along, its original point lost in translation. They were discussing typhus and bubonic plague and cholera, their differences and effects. Sometimes they did this in relation to imaginary flocks of animals, sometimes they would be in the Middle Ages in a castle, talking of the peasants.

"The epidemic that caused the fall of Rome—"

"—all that we are not we owe the louse, the flea, and the rat."

Nell watched a fight at the wicker bar across the room. It was real, and so stood out in the Parrott.

A woman in a red halter had turned her back on the man with her, a husband, and was showing off a tattoo on her shoulder to a delighted drunk who craned for a look at her breasts.

Nell watched the threesome. Her sympathy was with the husband. But as she moved to rise, she knew it was not him she went to get.

Lightly she touched Woody's shoulder to let him know she was leaving, and gathered up her things. She felt a sense of having waited the past six years to look up across this crowded room. And now that it had happened, she felt light and happy. Strange that you never knew how lonesome you had been until the time was past.

"Hello there," she said to the short, red-haired man at the bar.

"Join the crowd," he said.

The couple looked at her warily; the woman resentful of her intrusion, the man relieved at the interruption.

"Don't you remember me?" she asked the agreeable drunk. "Years ago you sold a pint of blood to buy me an orchid for the prom."

He turned to her and grinned. "I think I sold your orchid for a pint, honey."

"Let's go have a drink and try to remember which it was."

"Sounds good to me."

"My name is Nell." She took him past the table with Woody and the group, out into another smaller room, an alcove where they could not be seen. The crowd would love it; it would be conversation for months, when the other games ran out. The night Nell, of all people, who would have thought, their original, cool as a cucumber, went over and picked up a stranger at the Parrott bar.

"What's on your mind, Nell? You don't seem the type to be rescuing a damsel in distress. She was asking for it."

"I wanted you myself. It seemed a waste, all that attention on a tattoo."

He looked at her when they had sat down and got a drink. "Imagine that, I've been picked up."

"What's your name?"

"Max. Wilhelm Maxwell. Willie Max. Helmwell. Whatever pleases."

"What do you do?"

"I write for newspapers. I'm a west coast reporter."

"What's your real name?"

"Maxwell Baxter. Max Bax for short. Hell, what does it matter?"

"I see you know Santa Fe."

"You're sulking and we've barely met."

"I like to know the name—"

"All right, Nell. Maximum Million. Maximillian. Why did you want me?"

"I don't know. Where are you staying?"

"On the square, a good newsman, at the ready for news."

"Come home with me, then."

"What about your friends?"

"What about them?"

"You trying to get even with the fag in the ruffled shirt or something?"

"No."

"I need another drink."

"I have gin at home. Take one with you and let's go."

"You got a tattoo?"

"I'll paint one on if you like."

"You mean I got picked up by a painter?"

He passed out on her white bed. They had not made love. Nell was anxious; she might have handled bringing him here, to her place, if they had been quick and drunk and caught up in the attraction she had felt when she saw him. But to wake up with someone you didn't know was frightening. She faltered and began to think of coffee, and herself dressed and at the canvas.

He woke, almost laughing. "Well, well," he said. "So this is what I have got myself, is it?" He helped her get out of her gown and made it easy for them to touch by talking about it in a bantering tone: "Well, now, I think I'll just have my way with you." After a while he entered her almost casually after a lot of kissing and searching around for possible good locations for a tattoo. Nell's fright had vanished. "My name is Max Short, and I am," he said somewhere in the undressing. It all seemed easy and funny, as if they were watching themselves do what everyone in the world did and enjoying that fact; the fact of knowing that it didn't have to be something unique and monumental, that it was amusing and pleasing that it was so ordinary. "Pretend we're in Mexico and there's a yellow dog lying outside the door, watchdog, and it's a hundred and three degrees, and your husband is expected back at any moment, and I've just started to pump when the dog gets kicked in the

73

head, and husband steps over the door jamb."

They lay sweaty a long time in her cool room, pretending one thing and another. "Do they call you Nellie?"

"No. It's LaNelle."

"My mother idolized a singer called Nellie Melba. I have all her records, seventy-eights, shellac. What a voice. Do you like that music? The old quartets? The old operas?" He touched her lightly. "I think I'll call you Nellie Melba. Nellie has a little belly."

"Do you want to know why I went across the room to you?"

"You can tell me why you think you did. I don't have to take your word for it."

"You look the way I remember my father."

He propped up on his elbow. "How was he in bed?"

"I haven't seen him since I was three. It isn't your face; it was something about the way you leaned across to that woman in the halter."

"You weren't one of those girls who was raped by their fathers?"

"No."

"Too bad. They excite me."

"My stepfather—bothered me a little." Nell observed her white room. "Will that do?"

"I'm only here for the night, Nellie."

"I had a marriage. Maybe I just want you for the night."

"Had one is good. I had one; I had a lot of it. In fact I only recently pried off the woman I had it with. I pried her off and she pried my son off. He's who's had it." He lay on his back. "How many kids you got? You got kids?"

"I have a son; he lives with his father."

"What'd the husband have on you?"

"That's what my mother said everyone would think."

74

"Everyone does."

"I didn't want to take him away; my husband had been raised without his father."

"You left your kid?"

"I fly back once a month to see him."

"I don't believe it, Nell. We're going to make you Queen of the Home for Lost Boys."

Later, when they got up and he had had a morning-after drink, he said: "Tell it to me again, Nellie, how you left your kid with his old man."

She showed him her present Dress. That is, she led him to it. As the space was small, the canvas huge, its model spread all over the table that served for studio not meals, it was hardly hidden. Better for him to make a comment now, and then if he did not understand, he would not have to speak of her painting again.

The pinkened Christening Dress, half finished, looked flat and wounded to her. It was not working, still. She had used yards of narrow rayon ribbons from the dime store and bits and scraps of old lace and linens for the body of it, and underneath, as petticoat, folds of tissue paper. She had placed tiny satin tinted flowers on the small puffed sleeves. She was driven crazy by the shade of pink that all light made of white in this place called Santa Fe. Pink crept under the doorsills, nestled in the darkest closets. She had done shadows of mars violet and brown madder alizarin, and light of jaune brilliant and flesh tint and rose madder and cadmium red, all thinned with zinc white, but those were names on tubes and not ever quite the light that fell on her flat, limp, giant Baby Dress.

"Jesus," Max said. "Did you do this? All these?" He gestured at the stack against the kitchen wall. "What are you doing hanging out with fags and dilettantes? I took you for society. In New York City you could get a grand apiece for these. What are you doing in this town?"

"It's invisible here," she explained. "I like that. Why are you here, a west coast reporter in Santa Fe?"

"Because there is no news. No war, no casualties, no napalm, no villagers on fire, no shot of nine hundred enemy soldiers lying in a sand dune trench, nobody talking about how our troops are all from the less privileged half of our society so what the hell that they die in droves. In Santa Fe I know all the barkeeps. I know the new places to go. I went to the Parrott last night for old times; but all the folks in the know have migrated to My Adobe Hacienda." He looked at her. "How come you and the fag weren't there? Don't you know what's new?"

She understood why he was in this town. It all mattered to him so much, his real world. He had to come for refuge to the place where nothing mattered. She smiled. "You do know Santa Fe. We were going to try the Adobe this morning."

He took a last look at her Dress and its model. "What do you call it when you pile it all over the table before you paint from it? I used to know the jargon. Facsimile? I learned words like *risible* and *emblematic*. I used to cover that stuff."

"I don't call it."

"Sartre says: 'Anything you name is already no longer the same.' "

"I haven't read that."

"I haven't either. That's the point, Nellie. This way we're both going to have the same misconceptions, and we can impress each other with our erudition." He turned from the Dress to her. "I'll buy you brunch at the Adobe. And wear a skirt, can you? You must have slept six weeks

76

in those brown pants."

"I'd like to make love again."

"Hello, Daddy . . . I may be better as an archetype."

"You may be."

"I may not can do it again."

"You may not."

"You may be working out your hostility against men by making me feel impotent."

"How powerful I am."

"You may be castrating me on the spot. Let's check and see." He laughed and pulled her close against him. "Nellie, see what you've done."

She laughed because she was happy. She looked at the short, red-haired man with the hairy barrel chest and the deep lines in his face and felt good. She wanted to lie on top of him with her panties on and have him take them off.

Which he did until he got it right.

It was late when they got to My Adobe Hacienda. But the crowd was there, lingering over gin and orange juice, excited to see Nell with her conquest. They went and sat with everyone. Max seemed quite at home. He was used to the sort of immediate air of intimacy that one gets with strangers in bars. He took Woody's hand and said, very jovially, "You must have been hell in bed, son, to make a woman that demanding."

Everyone was delighted with this brazen approach. They pulled up chairs and made introductions and Woody beamed and bought everyone a round, and Nell found herself blushing at one point like a schoolgirl in a brown coat who is out with her fellow. When cold spinach soup had been served and mayonnaise chicken, and a wine cooler that no one had ever had before was delivered courtesy of the house, and Bernie, the owner, was doing his Carmichael version of "As Time Goes By," Max whispered: "Was that okay?"

"You seem to know what works."

"Long training."

"I have learned here that being invisible is more a matter of conforming than disappearing."

" 'The Purloined Letter.' "

"I haven't read that."

"I haven't either."

Max had eight drinks with lunch. He was soon fast friends with all the crowd, and seemed to know Luciana already. He took Nell by the arm when it was time to go. "If you don't see Nellie for a while she hasn't been ambushed in the Cathedral. I may take her to L.A. with me."

They were all impressed. Woody said: "I should have thought of travel; an original artist needs a change of scene." And Nell gave him a kiss on the cheek so that everyone would be comfortable.

Alone with Max, she said, "I can't paint in L.A."

"Who can paint in L.A.?"

"Do you always drink that much?"

"Yes."

Nell held onto his fingers. They were walking down a dusty side road to the river. "What do I do about that?"

"My ex- talked about it a lot."

"No, I mean—if I get involved."

"Aren't you? You've been sullen and castrating. You must be involved."

"Then how do I handle it?"

"I thought you handled it like a pro."

"Your drinking."

"Pretend you're living with Dr. Jekyll and Mr. Hyde."

78

"I haven't read—"

He stopped her. "Don't, please don't, talk about it, Nellie Melba."

They went out to late dinner at Lucia's, a tiny, wildly expensive French place that took reservations a month in advance. And not from just anyone.

Max knew the owner, an old friend he said, whom Nell wondered if he had slept with some time back.

They encountered a waiter.

"Do you have a reservation, sir?"

"I'm a guest of Madge's."

"Madame didn't inform me."

"Inform her. Max Short."

He had brought Nell to the café not to impress her with its exclusive pose, but because the room was white. "I thought you'd like this," he said. The walls were whitewashed, with no paintings. Each white molded plastic pedestal table held one white peony in a cut glass vase. The chairs were wood, painted. The floor was marble. On the only windows, in the back, white heavy cotton draperies shut out the heat and the night.

"Jesus, Max, it is too beautiful."

"It's your place, right?"

"I love it that she hasn't hung any art. In a town that exists on art—the blank walls. And no plants. What is she like?" She felt jealous of a woman who could make space so incredibly fine.

"I don't know. I've only met her once. I got a niece of hers out of trouble by providing an alibi. A case of being around when someone needed to be around."

"I thought you were close to her—"

"We're all close in Santa Fe."

"What happened to the niece?"

"Her husband dumped her anyway. But the other guy got out of it, which was the point. You've probably heard the story."

They were at a small back table. Nell tried to order everything white: cold potato soup, filet of sole, hearts of palm, vanilla mousse. To make it perfect with the setting. She was delighted with being there, with having found Max, with the room, which was very special—something she could not have imagined, but, having seen it, wished she had.

Max had been drinking gin. Doubles on ice. He began to get louder. He told her that her paintings would bring a grand apiece in New York City. He talked about a woman who would leave her kid to his old man. He held her hand.

The people at the next table left. Nell ate her sole and drank the Chardonnay. She watched Max get more voluble, and less aware of where he was. It must be that drinking took you from the present entirely and set you down somewhere else. Somewhere that you fought all the rest of the time not to be. Maybe he was in the same place, or maybe he was not, as when the woman in the Parrott bar was unbuttoning her red top for him.

"I'm through, Max." She pushed the dessert away. "I love this place. I'm glad you brought me."

"What's your hurry? I can't even get this cretin to bring me the check much less a cup of coffee." His words were slurred.

Nell signaled the waiter, who took Max's American Express card. Helplessly she looked on as Max tried to sign his name. She should have done that for him. It was unreadable. Maybe that was all right. They knew him. Perhaps the imprint of the credit card number would do and any scrawl at all, even an *X*, was all that was needed.

They had got to the door when the waiter came rushing up to them. "Surely, sir, you intended to leave a gratuity? Was the service not good, sir?" The bill had been for sixty-two dollars. Max had left the line for the tip blank. She should have tucked ten dollars under her plate. This was new to her. She could see, but too late, all the things she could have done to cover him: but she had not comprehended it in time. She had been transfixed by the stark, white room.

Maybe they would not eat out at night. That would be all right. Night could be soup and cheese at home. It had been gay and safe at the Adobe for lunch, with everyone there. That was the point of going out, after all, to blend with the crowd and appear like them. You didn't need to do that every day; you didn't need to go out at night.

Max smashed the waiter's face with his fist.

Nell thought she was going to pass out. Dear God, what did you do?

"Call Madame," she said to another waiter nearby. When an imperious woman appeared, Nell said, "Max hit your waiter. Here is a twenty for his tip. I'm getting him out of here. I don't know what else to do."

"Henry will be okay," the woman, Madge, said calmly. "I forgot. I'm tired. I have not been sleeping. It was a hard week, my cook—never mind. I should have thought to tell Henry to make the dinner complimentary. Yes, of course. Max has made trouble before. But we're family here. I can do as I like."

A cab appeared, so that Max did not have to drive home.

"What the hell, a taxi in this town, what do they think this is, New York City? What the hell happened to the car? What the fuck . . . ?" His voice trailed off.

"Driver, thank you." Nell started to pay the man, but he signaled that it was taken care of.

In her studio room she got Max to bed, and he was out, or asleep, or whatever the state was when he was gone wholly and totally from where he was.

She sat on the side of the bed and thought about Lucia's. (Why, if the woman was called Madge, was the restaurant not named for her?) It was so beautiful; she had not had a chance to tell her. She went over it all again in her mind. The whiteness, the bare walls, the simple tables. She looked at her two rooms and tried to imprint the calm and elegance of the other white room onto these. She fell asleep beside Max with the image of a single white peony before her.

He came every week. Nell worked when he was on the coast; when he was here she did nothing but be with him. All their time was rose-colored time: the lavender shadows of adobe church altars, pink crushed strawberries for brunch, the ruby reds of sunsets seen from her bed.

All their time was full of joy for Nell.

Middays, they met the crowd. Mostly at My Adobe Hacienda, where Bernie, the owner, had taken them in as his first set of regulars, and played "As Time Goes By" whenever they appeared. He had taken a fancy to a painfully thin girl in their group, and coaxed her to sit beside him on the piano stool. She smoked incessantly; they called her Incessant Cecily, and she turned pages for him, blowing smoke, resting her head against his shoulder. The interior of the Adobe was chocolate checks and melting candles and baskets of red geraniums. They sat at wooden benches along a wall eating cold soup with homemade bread, or they sat wedged close to the piano at the bar. In either case all the seats formed a curve around the caged birds and platform where Bernie sat singing to them.

They sat with Woody and Luciana and her beautiful man with the crumpled ear. (Once Nell had suggested to Luciana that he was Woody's lover, but this had angered the gallery owner: "The proof of the pudding . . ." she had said curtly. Nevertheless, Nell knew that it was true.) And things fell into place as Nell pieced together that Luciana was Madge's niece—therefore the reason for the restaurant's name, and the way Max knew her. It all fit together when you knew, in Santa Fe.

"Why does the crowd never go to Lucia's?" she asked Max.

But, as he explained, she could see that the point was to know the connection but to never mention it; not to go there but to know that any time you wanted to you could.

She and Max did not go again. At night they brought home a sack of food, or she fixed soup and fruit, and they ate early, and then climbed up on Nell's white bed and talked until Max drifted away. She wore a long brown terry robe, tied at the waist; and moved aside the row of glass-eyed china baby dolls that lived with her, to make room for Max. He always ate with her—a good influence, he said—but then took his gin and glass and lay on his back, propped up, and told her all about his life or pried into hers.

"What do Mom and Tom think about your carrying on with a forty-year-old Jew?"

"Are you?"

"The first, for sure. The second is rumored. My grandparents claim it: they changed their name to Short, for short, when they came over. My parents deny it; they are registered Unitarians. All I know for sure is that I don't know for sure."

"I haven't told my family anything except that there is someone. They like to think of me alone. It justifies Alfred staying behind."

"Remember, you're the Queen of the Home for Lost Boys."

Sometimes he put his head in her lap, when he had begun to lose his words, and talked about his parents. Primarily, his father's shop. His having to learn to refinish furniture, and hating it. The lye-like smell of the stripping compound that stung the nostrils. His hands blistered. His nails dirty from the stain of the varnish, and his neck from the sander's dust. "Hell is refinishing furniture. It is a sign in your front yard: ANTIQUES AND BARGAINS. *Blackberry Jams. Damson Jellies. Best in the West.*" He hated most his father—passing the glued, caned, stained, nailed pieces off as heirlooms.

At the last, as he faded off, he recited poetry. Scraps of poems that he had made into a ritual recitation. "I've read that," he would say. "I've damn sure read that."

He started with Yeats:

> "*I will arise and go now, and go to Innisfree*
> *And a small cabin build there, of clay and wattles made;*
> *Nine bean rows will I have there, a hive for the honeybee . . .*"

Then, Sandburg:

> "*Mamie beat her head against the bars of a little Indiana town and dreamed of romance and big things off somewhere the way the railroad trains all ran . . .*"

84

And:

"I drank musty ale at the Illinois Athletic Club with the millionaire manufacturer of Green River Butter one night . . ."

He would digress: "Now what more do you need? Drinking ale with the millionaire manufacturer of Green River Butter. That ought to be enough for one lifetime, wouldn't you say? For someone who's been scraping the fucking varnish off a chest of drawers for three days and is covered already with forty years of stain."

Max's cleanliness was, she guessed, a reaction to this father. He showered three or four times a day, and each time he put on a fresh shirt. Not the Mexican shirts or t-shirts the crowd wore, but dress shirts; white, pink, blue, cream, he had a dozen with him on every trip. He would sweat through one, take it off drenched, shower, and put on a clean one. "I hate looking like a tramp. Newspaper men are tramps. They don't shave for weeks. It's the War Correspondent fever; they all think they're Mauldin at the front. I want to look like I'm in business. Selling shoes." (He wanted to look, she knew, as though it didn't matter.) He ended, always, with lines from James Stephens:

> *"Song, I am tired to death! Here let me lie*
> *Where we have paced the moving trees along!*
> *Till I recover from my ecstasy,*
> *Farewell, my Song!"*

"I read that—" And he would roll over and be gone; asleep or in the place the liquor took him.

And Nell beside him would be there, and nowhere else; nowhere but with Max when he was in her bed.

* * *

85

Having Max in her life did not change her times with her son; but it brought new anger to her conferences with Tucker, his father.

"Hello, Alfred."

"Hello, Mother."

They continued to meet at her wood half-house in San Antonio. If Alfred stayed over, which he sometimes could now if they went to a movie, he stayed upstairs in the wobbly pebble gray-floored room. He was not allowed to fly to Santa Fe to see her; so Tucker paid her plane fare back home.

Her son was a tall ten-year-old. He was neat, sandy-haired, hazel-eyed, mannerly, diffident. She searched his face sometimes when she had not seen him for a while, to see if the infant she had known best was there somewhere. It was awkward to be formal with someone you had given birth to; but less so if you had been that way from the start.

"Do they call you Al?"

"Dad does. Aunt Mo calls me Alamo." He looked embarrassed but pleased. "For Al and Mo. That way she says she won't *forget*." He looked at his mother to see if she got it.

"Let's take our walk," she offered.

Sure enough the dogs appeared, bounding, as if they had been doing this every morning for all those years. Fred, the aging basset, Shred, the sagging many-teated mama, Red, the anxious setter who had grown scatter-brained and sometimes leapt up on strangers, and Teddy, the fat, sweet golden retriever—their favorite. "Come on, gang," Nell said, giving the whistle again that had called them forth.

"She looks like her name is Fed." Alfred laughed at his joke.

86

"Fat Feddy." They smiled at the golden lab.

Her son ran a little ahead with the dogs and then waited for her. "Sometimes at school we call each other names. My girlfriend at school is named Astilbe, and we call her Silly, but it makes her cry. And Godfrey, he's my best friend, we call him Hot Fries. But not when his mom is there."

"What do they call you?"

"Alley Cat." He turned red. "It's a kind of joke."

After a block or so, she said: "You have on new shoes."

"They're Adidas. I'm taking tennis lessons."

"Do you like to play?"

He frowned. "Grandmother is giving me lessons."

"Grandmother Drury?"

"Grandmother Estelle."

Nell liked that. She pictured Mommy sitting in crisp white shorts and shirt at the tennis club, having an excuse to be there with her young grandson, looking trim and tan, sitting with a group of young mothers.

"Your father is a fine player," Nell offered.

Alfred did not answer. He did not like to talk about his other parent to this one. She was not sure whether it was that it was painful, or that it was ambiguous. It would be hard for a ten-year-old to know what the right tone and stance was for such matters.

"Is it hard for you," she asked, "my visits back?"

He trudged along on his thin straight legs. The dogs running back and forth around him. "Dad says I am to be friendly to you."

"He's thinking about his mother. You don't have to be any way to me you don't want to."

"I don't mind," he said in a muffled voice.

"I know it feels bad to have somebody who should be there not there. I didn't have my daddy growing up; your father didn't either."

"Are you getting even?" His face was red and he didn't look at her.

Nell stopped in front of an old house. The question caught her by surprise. "I don't think so," she said uncertainly. "I think I wished I had not lived with my mother. I don't know what that means about you and me." Was every parent who left a child getting even? Was Max? Had her father been? Was she? If so, at whom? The parent who raised you or the one who didn't?

"Are we going to get a hamburger?" Alfred asked.

"I may get eggs."

They walked down through the smaller houses with the larger trees, leaving the pack of dogs sighing in the grass, awaiting their return. They ate at the café with the ruffled curtains and the efficient waitress.

Nell thought about her father and the scene she had longed for: Belle Watling, empty whiskey bottles, disorder on the floor. It was time for Alfred to be offered another view of life. Time he saw what one left for. That was only fair.

The boy was sent up to bed when she took him home. Tucker did not like the two of them to visit in front of him. "That's asking too much, Nell."

"May I sit down?"

"You want a drink? It's late."

"I want Alfred to come visit me in Santa Fe."

"I thought we had settled that. He's too young to handle what he might see out there. It's no place for children."

"Then I want Max to come here. I want Alfred to see the reality of my life."

"I will not permit Alfred to be in your home with one of your lovers, Nell."

"I don't have plural, Tucker. I am serious about Max. He is a journalist; he has a son of his own."

"If you have overnight company here, we will simply skip that weekend. Alfred thinks you left because you wanted to live alone. That is what I convinced myself. It would destroy the good image I have tried to give him of you, if you had someone sleeping at your place. Surely that is obvious."

"I hate lying to people under six feet tall. It makes me sick." She drew in her breath. She had tied her hair back and put on a brown skirt, in order to appear a conventional mother for this conversation. "What do you say to Alfred about other people?"

"What do you mean?"

"Who you are dating. Does he see her? Does she spend the night?"

Her former husband got up and walked to the fireplace. He rested his arm on it lightly, to give himself a feeling of ownership in his house. He had on a tennis shirt with an alligator trademark and shorts with a buttoned pocket flap. At ten o'clock at night. "I think," he issued a considered reply, "that I have been as careful about that as is possible. I felt there was no need to upset Alfred any more than was inevitable in the circumstances, no need to accustom him to further loss."

"You dated behind his back." She refrained from saying screwed.

"I have been discreet. Now, however—"

"Now?"

"I have been seeing Amaryllis Smith. Her daughter Astilbe is in Alfred's class. It is natural, we think, to both children, that we get together for meals or outings. Much as one would do with friends and their children in the normal course of events. She never stays overnight, needless to say."

"Alfred said today that Astilbe was his girlfriend. Don't you think—"

"I'm sure when he said that he meant that she was a friend. He's only ten years old, Nell. Don't project your morals on him. At any rate, that is as far as we wish to go at this point where the children are concerned. Amaryllis and I have discussed marriage; and, if it comes to that, I'm sure it will seem a very natural thing for both children."

Nell felt miserable for her son.

"I feel," Tucker added, "it would be better if the grandmothers resumed dropping him off and picking him up. I don't think it helpful for Alfred to see us together. He is always moody for a few days after."

Small privileges were being removed. Perhaps Mommy had had this conversation with Nell's daddy. You may do this and never this and only sometimes that. One day he must have broken his heart, and moved on. She could understand. Possession was nine parts of parenting. For the rest, it cost a lot for what you got, or gave.

All love, she considered when she was alone, must cost the same. As she had fought those years in Santa Fe to make cool colors on her canvas, so also she had fought its languor and indolence to retain some passion inside her. Now in her joy at having found it with Max, she saw that she had forfeited the regimental order that had constituted her life before him.

Still, it was worth the price. It was time for Nell to be offered another view of life. It was time to see at last what one stayed for.

Nick

◆

"YOU'RE GOING TO WALK UP to the platform to get your Nobel Prize and they'll ask your family to stand and guess what—there'll be no family. It will be too late. I'll be dried up or washed up, if I haven't given up by then."

They were in Santa Fe for their twelfth wedding anniversary. Nicholas had set aside a week, without his daughters, away from the lab. Joey and Johnnie, now 7 and 8, were old enough to leave behind with the sitter who fed them and got them to and from school and turned on and off the television set. One night they would be driven to Kansas City to eat with their grandparents, who now took them for limited, scheduled appearances. ("You sweet dears," his mother would start, "now don't you look like, although that isn't true, your father and my youngest, your uncle Richard, when they were your—")

He had promised Virginia that this trip would be for pleasure. He was to empty his mind of work; they were to sleep late, drink lots, see the sights, and make love "the way we used to." But even as he had gone for two days through the motions of play, Virginia had become angered and bitter. Things were no different, she said. They could have saved themselves the fifty dollars a night for the elegant

Spanish colonial suite with the plaster walls, and cluttered Indian markets and noisy tourists on the square below. "You might as well have spent it on your rats."

She was correct that he had been thinking about the lab since they left home. He had read *The Double Helix* on the plane and found what he had expected: that the nine-hundred-word original article in *Nature*, about the structure of deoxyribonucleic acids revealed as a copying mechanism for genetic material, had been reported as a heated track meet, with the author as the winner. That must have felt hurtful to others who had been themselves working on the discovery: Linus Pauling, Edwin Chargaff, Rosalind Franklin. He did not know how they felt, but Nicholas still had a nagging doubt that the double helix was the only model that would fit the original X-ray diffraction data. It had seemed to him too hasty: a conclusion made with the prize in mind. As serious a fault was that the reporting contained no sense that nothing is a separate discovery, that everything builds on what went before, that who plugs the lamp into the wall is as important as who turns on the light.

No doubt readers would construe the discovery to say that humans are what DNA makes to replicate itself—a doctrine of predestination that the Presbyterian church could envy. Nicholas, however, hoped to find in it the opposite conclusion: a theory implying that choice was in fact at work in the universe somewhere by something. Lamarck had been resurrected by the genetic transmission of the DNA molecule.

Nicholas' mind was never off his research, although more and more his job had come to take time away from his work. His colleagues in the field used the knowledge that the chemistry of the brain altered its electrical activity to treat mental patients with increasingly effective drugs. He could not fault that. But it seemed remedial work—to give palliatives to further alter states that had been already considerably altered. And though he was glad that it was now possible to mitigate pathological symptoms enough to enable schizophrenics to become Chamber of Commerce vice-presidents, that was not his goal; he still sought to prove that changes could be made and transmitted to the next generation by discretely permeating the membrane controlling the genetic pool. The question was how, and under what conditions.

Last week Nicholas had gone to hear a talk by a physicist named John Wheeler, who said a sentence that lingered in his mind: *In an empty courtyard we are playing a game which cannot be played until someone draws a line.*

He could not stop thinking of that. It seemed to him the clue. He must be drawing the line in the wrong place.

"What do you want me to do?" Nicholas asked Virginia, now, in their hotel bedroom. He longed to take some action to get them off the old, sore dispute.

"If you want the truth, for you to put me first, for the five days we've got left. That's all, five days."

"Would you like to rent a car and drive up into the mountains? Do you want to talk about your going back to school? Do you want to talk about where we are?"

"If you have to ask, if you have to ask what it means to put a woman first—it's like they say, if you have to ask what it costs you can't afford it. You just can't do it, can you?" She stepped out of her gown. She was still lovely, although her beauty had taken on a puffy look. "I want you to want it. Can't you remember back to Cleveland? You wanted it then. Do you remember then? What did we talk about? Before the rats? What did you think about, before the rats, up in your precious ivy school?"

He answered her carefully, but truthfully. He knew it would spark more trouble, but he could not let it go, as it was the point of their discord. "In school I wanted to find work; that's why I was there."

"Richard said you were a grind from the word go."

"He's generally correct in his assessment."

"About me, you mean." She grabbed at her clothes and held them against her for cover. "What would it take to get through to you in a woman, anyway? Not someone who really exists, some fantasy—" She slammed the door into the bathroom.

Nicholas sat thinking about Virginia's question. What I want, he admitted slowly, is a woman like Dr. Cavender's wife.

He had got up his nerve the summer before he went off to college to call on the man who had once confronted his mother about the mahogany table. It was foolish the importance that that night had had for him, but its impact had not diminished. He had in his mind somewhere the notion that if he saw the man again, and listened to his voice, that some necessary secret would be revealed; that he, Nicholas, could leave home in possession of more than the puzzle that had constituted his education in the library at his parents' house, and at the hands of his brother.

"Sir," he had said uncertainly into the telephone, "this is Nicholas Clark. I wonder if I might come pay a call on you?" How awkward and formal he must have sounded.

At the door he was met by the psychoanalyst, who looked exactly as Nicholas had remembered, so vivid was the impression he had made. "Come in," Dr. Cavender said in welcome. "Maisie, this is Francis Clark's son."

His hand was clasped by a plump little woman who scarcely came up to his chest. "Your father is a fine surgeon," she said graciously.

Nicholas' reaction had been surprise; he realized that he had always taken his father's own low estimation of himself as truth. "Thank you," he said, as he made note of this new perspective.

Mrs. Cavender led him into a cluttered sitting room. "Sit down, Nicholas. Will you have coffee with us?"

"Yes, Ma'am." He did not want to refuse, but he did not want to send this warm direct little woman into the kitchen to get anything for him.

He need not have worried; that was not her task. "Edward will get us something," she said pleasantly. "I have only this moment come from the lab and it will take me a few minutes to unwind." She took off her shoes and leaned back with a sigh. "It takes a while for me to forget about my oats—" She sketched for him briefly her experiments under infra-red light.

He had listened in embarrassment. He had thought of her as *Mrs.*; it seemed impossible to call this motherly dumpy woman *Dr.*, although apparently she was.

Dr. Cavender carried in a tray that contained pound cake, coffee, real cream, and, in a measuring cup, brandy. He explained that the cake, which was still in its tin pan, had a special crust of lemon juice and sugar that he used to jazz up storebought sweets, and that the measuring cup was so you did not either appear miserly with guests or sock them with twice what they could manage.

Nicholas found it all strange and very comforting: the genuine hospitality, as well as the direct explication of what they were about to eat.

After he had had cake, and been warmed with an unaccustomed ounce of brandy in his coffee, Nicholas got up his nerve to mention the night he had met Dr. Cavender.

"Your mother had changed a great deal," the analyst reported.

"Did you know my parents, sir, before?"

Dr. Cavender hesitated a moment. "Your mother I knew years ago. Not your father."

Nicholas wanted to pursue that, but did not feel he was supposed to. He waited, but no more was said.

"Tell us," Mrs. Cavender asked after a slight pause, "are you in college now, Nicholas?"

"I will be this fall—at Harvard." He had been angered at himself for adding that, for having been so influenced by his father's values that he said it to these people. For what struck him the most about them, although he had not the concept then for it, but only the impression, was that they were exactly the same with him as they were when alone together or separately. This contrast with his parents stirred in him an almost desperate response. "For my Dad," he added, sure that made no sense to them.

"Well, you must report back to us how you like it," Mrs. Cavender said mildly. She and Dr. Cavender talked back and forth then about their own college days together in Michigan.

After a time Nicholas was gently dismissed. "Maisie and I always have our nap when she gets home from the lab," Dr. Cavender said. He held out his hand. "But you must come again."

To Nicholas then, that boy, the older couple's marriage

had seemed the perfect life: for each to go to work and then to come home and lie down together.

It seemed so still, to Nicholas grown.

He talked often to Virginia about her going back to school or back to work. Not admitting to himself the fact that you could not go *back* to a place you had never been; or that it was his pressure on her, not her interest. Their needs worked in opposition to one another. He wanted her to have work and she fled from it; she wanted to be desired and he grew hesitant.

It was as if his body had begun to draw away from her, the way lumbering things are always found alone. Now when he did touch her in the bed, he felt awkward, as if he were not fast enough, or eager enough; as if he had backed too far away and by the time he got there she would be gone. Her body still moved him; he could still touch her shoulder and recall all that went with it. But the magic seemed sealed away, separate, and less and less often did he let it out; more and more he began to fear her ridicule of him.

Part of that must go with the knowledge that other men had been with her. When he thought about that, which he avoided doing, he told himself it was her revenge for what she felt was his own infidelity: the lab. But nonetheless, it affected him. He knew he had become slower, less sure, less spontaneous. It took longer and longer to move his desire from the past into the present with her.

"Let's don't fight," he said to her when she reappeared. "Let's go down to brunch," he offered when she did not answer. "We can take a walk. See the galleries and shops if you like. Then we can come back up and take a nap; the

98

whole town shutters down in the afternoon heat." He was promising what she wanted. "I want it to be a good week for us."

"I hate those miserable Indian women, squatting out on the sidewalk like flies, selling their miserable turquoise." Virginia got angry at the sight of the impassive Indian women who had set up tables and spread blankets of wares, jewelry mostly, on the covered porch in front of the Governor's Palace.

The city sold itself in that way on every street corner. He imagined that even in the seventeenth century the priests had sold olive-pit rosaries from the Mount of Olives to the Indians—who had sold them back cornshuck dolls.

"What else can they do?" he asked Virginia.

"That's the question I ask myself." She turned away. "About myself."

Her yellow dress moved with the motion of her hips, but she had the pinched look that her face got when she had the first indication of a headache: as if she could squint it out, like a cinder in the eye.

He did not want her to get a migraine on this anniversary. If she spent the time in bed, she would go home angrier than she had come.

As he watched her teeter gingerly around discomfort, aiming at all costs for avoidance, a comparison came to him concerning her headaches and his work. When she hurt in that way it was not possible for her to think of anything else, as pain, by its nature, was a signal that overrode all others. It was a matter that forced the mind's exclusive attention.

He touched her arm. "Come walk in the shade." He led

her to an alcove made of huge wood beams and adobe. "If you could think of the lab as the same for me as your head-ache is for you—"

She looked as if he had struck her. "You're saying my head being split in two is the same as one of your goddam Norway rats being shocked in his electric chair. I don't believe it." She stepped blindly into the sun and the street. "You'll bring it on," she screamed. "You saw this goddam glare get to me so you decided you could get rid of me for the rest of the trip. Sock me down with the pills you spend your time inventing."

He could see where this was leading. They would go back to the room. She would say it over and over again until he gave up and retracted his words. She would cry until she had extinguished it. And then, when the fight had subsided, they would make love; and he would have to do so with enough ardor and in a way that made her feel that he could not resist her. He would need, finally, to as-sure her that his mind was nowhere else, or, rather, that (for she thought of mind and body as severed, distant kin, as in the case of her headaches) he had given his mind over to his body's need for her. And then they would go down-stairs to a café or bar; and the sort of cheerfulness that came over her with the aftermath of a fight would settle in. She would be gay, demonstrably so.

He did not want to go through that on this particular afternoon. What if he did not go up with her, but instead continued his walk? Would it break the pattern or did you have to have the fight eventually in any case?

"I'm going back to the hotel," she said, her teeth clenched.

"I'll be up later." He looked at the sidewalk vendors.

"You won't find me there, then." She turned and he

watched her yellow dress sway across the crowded street.

The light did hurt the eyes. Although it was no hotter than Kansas in the summer, it was too bright. It was this quality of too much light that made one search out the shadows and the cool places. The adobe buildings lent themselves well to the sun's blaze; they were constructed to combat it, with their thick walls and wide porches.

He went into a shady café filled with enough lush foliage to be a greenhouse. He hoped Virginia would not come in after him, dry-eyed, heavily made up, and distant. Not until he had eaten and rested his eyes.

"You having lunch or breakfast?" A pretty waitress stood with her weight on one leg, waiting.

He smiled at thinking of *waiting* in that new way, and at her, and ordered coffee and a strawberry waffle. He felt foolish, as he had eaten the same thing earlier, but decisions did not appeal to him at this time. The waitress was too thin, and, under a lot of glued-on eyelashes and red cheeks, was obviously much younger than she was pretending to. He found her exceptionally attractive.

He gestured toward a nearby table of handsome people in bright clothes. "Who are they?" He did not care; he wanted to keep her there.

"Artists, more than likely." The girl made a face. She shifted her weight to the other leg.

"Painters?"

"I bet about two of them paint. The rest just hang around and call themselves artists. I bet they're rich folks who can afford to live in this town and not work. That's not me. It's high as a kite up here to live. I never see any of them doing anything." She had lowered her voice slightly; it had a nasality and looseness that he couldn't place regionally.

"Where are you from?" he asked.

"Around here." She looked vague. Perhaps she was a runaway. "I make jewelry myself."

"Do you sell it?"

"Consignment. Let me tell you those folks on the square make a mint. That turquoise is marked up, you wouldn't believe how much. I mean it. Michael, that's my boyfriend who used to work here at the Parrott, but he's at the Adobe now, told me how much it got marked up. Two hundred percent. Pictures are the worst. You can't touch nothing, anything, around this place in the way of art for less than five hundred. That's the tourist influence."

"Are you in school?" He wanted her to stay and talk.

"Not right now. I'm working here steady. I used to be. I guess I'll go back. When things aren't such a mess in the world. Michael says there's no point in getting educated, what is the point, at a time like this?"

"Tell me about your jewelry."

"It doesn't look bad. Listen, I got to go see about my tables. I'll get back here in a second."

He felt an overwhelming desire to listen to her talk about when she was in school and why she was in Santa Fe and what it was about Michael that made him her boyfriend. He felt an attraction to her that amazed him, and made him feel foolish. It was her accepting manner: Things were bad, but that was to be expected; things were good for the rich artists, but that was to be expected, too. It seemed simple. He wanted to watch her make turquoise bracelets and silver looped earrings. He wanted to watch her bend over, concentrating, not paying attention to him because she was busy making it come out right. Then he wanted her to pull off her cotton shirt and lie with him, but paying no attention to that either, simply doing it be-

102

cause it was siesta time, and natural.

He wanted to hear her say: "Look at this, Michael. Nicholas has come home with us, he has no place to go. I told him he could sleep on the pallet on the porch." He wanted to watch her undress and take a bath at the sink. He wanted to hold her; she was too thin.

With this unlikely fantasy, the full degree of his loneliness settled on Nicholas. He watched her slip through the greenery, pouring coffee, taking plates, keeping drinks refilled. Serving clumsy men their second cup of coffee. He wanted to know her name.

His isolation was increased by the constant laughter from the artists' table next to him. He could catch only snatches of lines and they made no sense at all. No one remark seemed to bear any relation to the one preceding or following it. It might as well have been a foreign tongue. Or was, in fact, to him. He could get no feel, either, for what they were to one another, whether couples or bare acquaintances. He felt excluded even from the ordinary observations one thinks it safe to make of strangers.

One of them, a woman, bent her head against the shoulder of the man next to her, and then looked directly up. She was striking, out of the ordinary, and, again, he felt a desire all out of proportion to the setting or the circumstances. He would like to have recognized the dark woman, waved at her, gone over to her table. He would like the artists to have looked up, laughed comfortably, and welcomed him. "Nicholas, long time no see. You missed a party Saturday; we missed you there. She missed you most of all." The woman would pull him into a seat by her, and they would all include him. And they would make sense to him.

He wanted desperately to belong to someone: the waitress and her Michael, even the table of idle artists.

At that moment he saw his wife leaning on a wicker bar in the corner. She wore a red halter half unbuttoned in the front, and had tucked a fresh flower behind her ear. The bare shoulders displayed the aquamarine butterfly—and her obvious availability.

Anger rose in him and he felt close to tears. She must have been there for at least the length of one drink, as her glass was empty and she was chewing a slice of lime, looking around.

He walked to where she stood. He considered and rejected several sentences, saying, finally: "The red is becoming."

She studied his face and tone for sarcasm. She was uncertain how to pursue a fight that had not taken place. She did not know what step to take next, and, seeing her uncertain, he relaxed somewhat.

She ordered, and got, another drink, turning her red pantlegs in his direction, so that the bottom half of her was toward him but the top half still leaned on the bar. She eyed the bartender, and bit her lower lip, trying to calculate her next move.

He wanted to say, "Let's quit and go upstairs," but felt he had forfeited that chance.

She had got herself in hand. "If you're not going to have a drink, there's no point in your standing there." She turned the long red pants away from him. Over her shoulder, she threw out: "Like a parole officer."

"Would you like to take a walk?"

"In these shoes?"

She had on, he saw, high-heeled sandals.

"Bring your drink to the table, then, I still have coffee—" He wanted to get them out of public view. He looked back to his small table, but could not see whether it had been cleared. The thin waitress may have taken his dishes and put on a fresh place setting. He realized that he had not left a tip. "Some people who you least expect it of are cheap," she would say to Michael. "I could of waited six tables in that same time."

"I didn't come to this bar with you—that was your choice, you may remember," Virginia had raised her voice. "I went up to the room alone, you weren't in the mood, you may remember." She touched a red nail to her shoulder, and ordered a third gin and tonic.

"I wasn't in the mood for a fight."

"You weren't in the mood, period."

A man came up to the bar on Virginia's left. He appeared to be already drunk. "What you got on your shoulder?"

"Take a look." She leaned in his direction.

"Fancy. You got any more?"

"Let's see." She leaned forward and unbuttoned another button on her halter, baring half her breasts.

"I've got one myself, from old Navy days."

"Show me." Virginia moved against his arm.

"It's here somewhere." He called for another drink. His words were indistinct.

The man had an air of confidence that reminded Nicholas of Richard—it was his assumption of attractiveness to women. It was clear in his face and stance. He pursued when it suited him; or did as long as he was on two feet. The question was never one of success. He was comfortable now, flirting in public with the half-dressed married woman, and would be equally able to move on when it appeared to be a bad scene.

On some level Nicholas felt pity for his wife. That she should need this to the degree that she was willing to stand

and beg some bystander for it.

He started to say her name, to let the man know he was with her, but found that he could not. Nicholas felt as out of control as if the man had indeed been his brother Richard.

"I need another drink, barkeep. You look real nice with that flower in your hair, doll." The man grabbed for his double gin refill.

Virginia touched his hand. "Show me your Navy tattoo—"

At that moment one of the artists came toward them, the striking woman with the dark hair.

Nicholas felt a loosening in his chest. He could not believe she was coming up to him, yet she seemed to be smiling in his direction. He wondered if it was a dare: Go rescue the guy and I'll buy you dinner. It did not matter. To move away from this scene on his awkward feet with someone like her seemed too much to hope for. He took a step in her direction.

"Hello, there," the woman said, walking past him and slipping her hand through the drunk's arm. "Remember me?"

"Be glad to." Clearly the man didn't, was hardly capable of it, but after a sentence or two, he went off happily with her.

As they left, Nicholas heard the dark woman say, "—with her husband standing there?"

"How'd you know that? They never said a word to each other."

"That's how you know."

"Now that you remind me—"

Then they were across the room, and gone.

Nicholas felt devastated. He had once again misread all

the cues; it felt like the afternoon of the gold birthday party.

"I'm going to bed," he said to his wife, who stood silently with her bare back to him. She could follow if she liked and enact the screaming reproachful fight. Or she could stay and try her luck again. He was past caring.

He did not turn as he left the room to look either at the laughing artists or at his own small table.

4

San Francisco

Nell

———◆———

N ELL SAT IN THE DARK.

It was finished.

Max slept heavily in his sweat-drenched pajamas. The sheets were soaked; earlier he had had a chill.

They were at his sister's house in San Francisco—a matching rust and buff and brown world of carpeting, draperies, sectional sofas, and wall plaques. It had been Nell's choice to come here rather than stay at a hotel, which Max could no longer handle. Family helped you out, she had reasoned, remembering Mo.

They had been in San Francisco before, once, shortly after they met. Max had wanted to bring his painter to the golden city, he said, where the sun lived. You have to see the light, Nellie, he had said. He did not mention a sister then; his tales of his family were confined to the house with the yard sign that said *Damson Jellies*. They had walked to the Evergreen Mortuary of McAvoy O'Hara, and then visited in turn Japanese, Filipino, Greek, and Russian tea rooms. He loved the name of the Mortuary, and resolved to leave it his remains. She said that back home they said that of the Bitters Road Dump. At twilight they had gone to a stretch of beach across from twisted cypress trees and a wide boulevard; gone down onto the sand and watched the sun fall into the sea, a great gold-red ball, suddenly swallowed, flooding the water with color. This thrilled them; they held hands in the sudden dark. It seemed then that the moon should rise and make a reflection as it swung, a yellow globe, above the sea.

Six years later that day was no longer possible.

She and Max had arrived yesterday, so that Max and Millie, who had not seen each other in a decade, could hug and make up, and put to rest their distance and distrust, before Nell's show.

"It's wonderful to see you, Max," Millie had said over and over. It meant she did not want to look at him. She did not know, for one thing, how an alcoholic would go over with her husband. They happened in the best of families, but, still, that might mean you had to be richer. She was not sure.

"I can tell it is," Max responded, kissing her warmly, then hugging her so close that she finally pulled away. "We were always close, weren't we?" He held his sister tight to feel her discomfort.

When Max had passed out, and she had got him to bed, the sister and her husband, Leo, talked somewhat more freely to Nell.

The brother-in-law made light of the situation. "Some of it's front, you know," he said. "An act. Newspaper men do that, drink hard, smoke hard; it's image. I wouldn't be surprised if half of it was an act." He read the paper, at his ease. He wanted his wife to know that she need not feel embarrassed, that having an alcoholic was more or less the same, statuswise and classwise, as having a politician in the family. You listened to them and knew that most of it was show. The only difference was that the politician got himself on the tube, but that could work against you.

"Do I call you Nell?" Millie asked in her buff and rust and brown living room, where they drank coffee on a plumped-up sofa. "He used some other name? I want to get it clear."

"Yes," Nell said. "Call me Nell."

Max called her Nellie Melba still. His stories of the singer varied. At one time he himself owned all the records of the greatest soprano who ever came out of a gramophone, who sang with all the famous, whose mad scene from *Lucia di Lammermoor* could not be equaled; at another he admitted that he had none of her recordings but had read about a man who possessed all 152. Sometimes it was that his mother had known her, or met her, or heard her sing—driving all night to the city. At others, that he had seen her picture once and liked the name. The point was the same: she was his romance. He wrote letters to Nell in Santa Fe addressed to Nellie Melba. If he sent white flowers for her room (if he was going to be gone too long) he sent them to: Nellie Melba LaNelle Woodard. For Short.

"I don't see how you stand it, Nell. I don't mean this to sound judgmental, or like I'm cutting down my own brother or something, I don't mean that at all. I'm certainly behind him all the way, at least I've tried to be, even though we're not in touch, you know. That's my notion of what family is. That's the kind of person I am. But, Nell, how do you do it? I'd be so edgy or something if someone was drinking all the time and I was close to them."

"We don't go out," Nell told her. "And haven't now for years." She could not tell it all to this sister with the buff-colored hair.

"What about tomorrow night? Your show?"

"If you and Leo would help out—"

"Well, sure, that's the kind of person I am. At least I mean to be. I guess I've always been jealous of Max. When we were growing up he got all that attention. Our daddy, I guess he told you, owned a furniture store with his brother, but we never had a nickel because my mother charged things all over town. When he died he left Mom up to her ears in debt, but that was her own doing. Whenever I needed fifteen dollars for some kind of lab fee or something —I was an all A student at that time—they'd make me work for it, in the store. But Max, they always had it for him. I guess I grew up jealous."

None of it fit damson jellies.

This morning over breakfast had been strained. Max had had a drink, but it had not yet caught up with him; he was tight as a drum. "Get Mildred to tell you about her cheer-leader phase," he said. "She was one swinger I can tell you. The boys took her over Pepsi Cola whenever they got the chance."

Millie and Leo, in brown velour robes, studiously read the newspaper. "Diane Keaton bought a fountain pen." Millie broke the silence. "They must be coming back."

"I see Teddy Kennedy made a trip to see his kid; that must mean he's going to run next time." Leo was a student of the political scene.

"I can't get scoops like that," Max said solemnly, helping himself to coffee. "What do you think of Nellie having a show in the city where the sun goes to bed? My Nellie. She could get a grand apiece for her stuff in New York City. You, sister, will be impressed as hell. Won't you? Or can you distinguish anything that doesn't match this department store decor?"

What Nell had forgotten was that for six years her life

had been dichotomy. When Max was in Santa Fe, she fit herself around his ways. When he was gone, her life and work resumed. They had developed routines, conventions, prohibitions of time and space of which she had ceased to be aware.

Some that still were difficult. They no longer made love; and Max did not know this. And had not for the last year.

In the beginning, those first months, he would wake her in the night, when he surfaced, and want her. And they would delight in it. Those were the best times.

Then, sometime later, a year or so, he began not to remember the nighttime sex.

One morning when he woke again he had asked her: "What are you doing in that gown?" She could not believe it. She had put on a new pink nightgown to celebrate that just finished Christening Dress; and had strewn pink flowers on the bed, and had pink champagne for ceremony. They had poured out the champagne and made love on the mound of flowers.

"You don't remember." It was not a question.

"We fucked?" He looked defensive. Then, after a minute: "It's not that it isn't good at the time, Nellie, don't you see, it's that afterwards it's gone, that's all, no recall."

After that, when he awoke, he would say: "Tell me what we did."

And she would describe it and that would arouse him and they would repeat it all. That time was good time, for his gratitude—that it did not bother her, that he did not have to lie—made him lavish in his offerings to her when he was awake and aware.

Later, when he no longer woke for the first time, she made up what she told him; gave him erotic make-believe

115

of what Max and Nell had done in the dawn on the floor or the bed. She would describe it—and they would act it out.

It had been only in the last year that he had heard the fantasies and not been able to respond. He had not been doing it twice for a long while; and now could no longer do it even once in the daylight.

Nell missed fiercely the times when he had thrown her on the bed, in Santa Fe or in his place in L.A., and she had clawed his back and kept her eyes open and had all she wanted. But what hurt the most was that he did not know it was gone.

Tonight was her first big show. A collector had seen her winter exhibit at Luciana's, where this year she had had the prestigious ski-season slot. He had called a friend on the coast. Nell sent slides; and the friend sent an offer.

It was to be, they explained, a four-woman show at the San Francisco Museum of Art. There were apologies for the sexism; but the truth was, it got more attention from the critics.

Luciana had done the selecting and packing. They had sent twenty canvases, variations on a theme: Convent Dresses, Communion Dresses, Christening Dresses. All set in the nameless village she had found high above Taos where mountains and forests blocked the slanting sun and shadows fell in blues and grays. Half stood in the nave of a small dimly lit chapel; half, in the glare outside against its whitewashed stucco walls or by its white wood cross in the courtyard. These cool canvases were her victory over Santa Fe. (Yet such a small graduating class for a dozen years' work.)

The museum had the same quality as Lucia's restaurant where Max first took her: the same composure, the refusal to pretend that all that is framed is art. She had the center spot, with ample space between each Dress for recovering from or anticipating the next. The show was in the wood-floored gallery; party food was in the vast marble rotunda across the hall.

She herself wore a white lace dress so there would be no mistaking that she went with the canvases. She carried a new china doll from her Babies Room as talisman.

She loved to watch the show-goers look and blink and turn to look again. She loved to listen in; they were not Friends, but pleasant strangers:

"I don't know about this stuff. My sister has a Jim Dine bathrobe, I mean an original, in her bedroom. But what does it mean, I said to her?"

"What I don't see is how you get any feeling without faces."
"That's stupid. You don't say that about abstracts."
"Maybe that's why I don't like abstracts."

"Honey, don't you think it's a little bit like that Andrew Wyeth print of the woman crawling in the grass?"

"They hurt my eyes."
"It says she's from Santa Fe."
"No, it says she's from Texas."
"That explains it. All you got there is sun. And dirt."

"It reminds me of that weird show we came for last year. What was his name? Nathan Oliveira. It's the same weird stuff."

"Well, he had a bunch of heads, remember? We could put them together. Wouldn't that be something? Mummy Face meets Baby Dress. Hey—?"

*   *   *

117

Nell saw it happen.

Max grabbed by the collar a strange man who had turned away, uninterested, to view another artist. "She could get a grand apiece for these in New York City," he shouted.

"Look, mister, I believe you. That's what they're marked, for God's sake. They're not my type, is all. Would you let—"

"I said one grand, do you hear?" He reached with his free hand for a waiter's tray, and crashed two dozen champagne glasses to the parquet floor.

As the waiter bent to move the pieces, Max swung his fist at the man who tried to get loose. "What kind of place is this, Nellie, where the hell? Did you hear, Nellie, this goddam cretin—" He slipped and landed on his back on the broken glass and wet floor. His clean cream shirt was streaked with blood.

"Oh, Nell, what are we supposed to do?" Millie and Leo rushed up to her, not wanting to claim kin in any way to the man on the floor.

"Miss Woodard, may we suggest—?" The director's assistant appeared.

"I'll take him home," Nell said to all of them.

She dropped her china doll.

She had been fifteen minutes at her show.

In the morning Nell offered reparation to Millie, who sat huddled on her buff couch. Humiliated, still.

"Let me take you to lunch," she said. "I'd like to do that. Let's go somewhere you've never been and have always wanted to go; that costs half a month's income. Some place where you have to have reservations and wait in line two hours to get in."

Millie let up a little. "There's a place I've heard about in

Marin County. It's a garden inside. The center is filled with a thousand tulips, can you imagine, or maybe it's lilies. They only have six tables for lunch."

"Let's take a chance and see if we can get in tomorrow. Before Max and I leave."

"If you really mean it, Nell." She inspected her nails. "I don't see how you stand it, honestly."

Nell and Max agreed to take one last look around. Sightsee the places they had been. Pay their respects to McAvoy O'Hara. Put the sun to bed.

They went to the redwoods. It was a long winding drive in Millie's sporty car with its brown and buff interior. But once outside on the ground with the fir high as the sky above them and the smell of needles beneath their feet it was fine. Especially the smell and the drab smoky greens.

" 'This is the forest primeval/The murmuring pines and the hemlocks . . .' " Nell quoted.

"I haven't read that," Max said.

"I did, once. 'List to the mournful tradition still sung by the pines of the forest.' "

"You're envious of my ability to quote unlimited verse."

"Mine is limited."

"Keep it that way." He put his arm on her shoulder. "My Nellie Melba mustn't know too much."

They talked about John Muir the naturalist, for whom the park was named. Max had a notion in his head that if you were a naturalist out in the wilds you had no need for alcohol. "I should have tried that," he would say, past tense. "One way or another man exiles himself from his fellows. That's a quote."

They walked the loop, climbing gently up through the trees, then arching and coming back down through them on the other side of a gully rooted with younger hardwoods. This forest had happened ages ago. Nell loved it and began to paint in her head. She envisioned Max's white shirt against a giant redwood. You could tell it was a tree only by the bark, for it made a dark background that shut out everything except the white flapping shirt. She remembered a fairy tale of the seven shirts and seven brothers, where the sister was to weave shirts for them so that they would no longer be birds but men again, but she didn't get the seventh finished in time, and one brother was left with one white wing. Nell could see the painting: the shirt, winged on one side, against the dark bark of another time.

A portrait of Max.

"Hemlock reminds me," he said, taking out his flask. "You have to drink in the city."

"This isn't city." Nell concentrated on the shirt, on how the wing would fit into it, on whether it should turn to the left slightly, favoring its cloth arm.

"Sure it is. You don't sell five hundred tickets a day to the country. Muir wouldn't be caught dead here."

"He was, I think."

"When he was here this wasn't here. It's city." Max argued for the sake of it.

They did that most of the time in places like this that were public. It was a way of talking that was not private, but was not making small talk. They would pretend to be a brother and sister having a feud over inheritance, or illicit lovers, or ex-spouses who have run into each other by mistake.

Sometimes when she fell silent, he would shout, "Argue, damn it," and she would make the effort. She tried now, but her voice came out flat and distracted. "Country can be crowded," she said. "That's not the point. You can have swimming holes and country picnics but it's still not city. City is streets and skyscrapers."

"What the hell? Where are you?" Max flew into a rage. He hated it when she went through the motions.

She could not fight as she used to. She knew it was because she was pulling away from him. At some point when he lost the mornings of love, and lost assignments, and lost track, and lost connections, she knew that he was lost. He knew it too—but they could not talk of it.

She had begun, she saw, to let him go. Distraction had set in, periphery began, tangential was in charge. "I was painting," she said.

"No wonder you forgot to participate; you forgot to be present this afternoon. I could be anyone in the world; west coast reporter returns to the scene of his crimes with a nellie who forgets he's there." Anger burst out.

Nell studied White Shirt with Tree. She noted carefully the way the feathers lay against the blackened bark.

Max quoted Sandburg:

" 'I wish to God I never saw you, Mag.
  I wish you never quit your job and came along with me.
  I wish we never bought a license and a white dress . . .
  Yes, I'm wishing now you lived somewhere away from
    here
  And I was a bum on the bumpers a thousand miles away
    dead broke.'

That's Nellie and white dress, miles from here," he said.

At the car he recited another;

" 'I say good-by because I know they tap your wrists,
  In the dark, in the silence, day by day.
  And all the blood of you drop by drop.

121

And you are old before you are young.
You never come back.'

That's Nellie who's gone." He did not speak all the way
back into town.

At the Evergreen Mortuary of McAvoy O'Hara, Max
opened the door and let Nell out. "Take your time. Take
a few hours. Go see your show. The creeps won't be there
since there's no free champagne. They don't give a fuck
about the pictures worth a grand apiece."

"Where are you going?"

"To see the sea."

"When shall I meet you?"

"Later." He looked out the car window. A wind was
blowing up the streets and down the hills. "Before dark.
Have yourself a tour. Get some tea." He closed the door.

"Let me go with you."

"Take your time."

Nell got out a guidebook that Millie had given her.
It relayed the information that up the hill behind the
mortuary were Japanese gardens and an Asian Museum.
Nell turned in that direction, trying to remember what
Chinese Year it was. Perhaps the Horse; there would be a
Ming display.

She climbed the hill slowly. People on this street had
tiny stoops no bigger than a passageway, gardens twice
the size of a shoe, small purple flowers and cropped box-
wood hedges in handkerchief displays.

She crossed a wide street and wandered through what
must be the Japanese gardens, as there were yew trees and
stately eucalyptus. To the right was an ornate pagoda; to
the left, a sidewalk led to the Asian Museum. Straight ahead

the land looked as if it fell away into a chasm. She went to see.

Below her, in a sunken park, was a grove of stunted trees. They were leafless and brown, planted in rows before an outdoor theater: a ghostly audience, listening to a silent concert. Nell read in her book that this was the band concourse between the museums of art and science; that the woods were pollarded trees, plane, elm, maple, walnut, and linden. Beneath the trees row on row of empty benches waited.

She walked down into the grove. The treetops were sheared off, leaving stunted sideways branches. At the top of the knobby protrusions sat motionless gulls—huge birds that looked too large for the bare flattened limbs. They seemed the size of chickens, three and four at the top of each tree; watchbirds that gazed without eyes in all directions, huge and cumbersome and unable to fly.

The concourse looked as if it were underwater, a deserted, submerged scene. As she walked deep into the woods she could see a difference in the trunks, some slick, others rough, some almost black, here and there a greened brown. But all were heavy around her and rose straight up through bare space to the strong deformed limbs that ended in birds overly gorged like tubers. It was dark among the trunks; the rows were hard to distinguish.

Ahead of her, just ahead, she saw a white lace Dress. It looked as if it were running, yet did not move. Its small sleeves puffed out as it turned to the side, listening to the sound of the concert from the stage.

She sat on a bench and put it through her eyes into her head: the gross birds stuck as if with chewing gum to the treetops, the forest, heavy and beheaded, the white Dress.

It was twilight and quite cool. The grays and browns made a monotone of the woods. She felt herself again the brown girl in the brown coat in the Kansas City train station. The bench felt as if it were the same bench. Trains arrived and departed but she did not move. She had followed the Dress to its lair; and she did not want to leave it. She shuttered it with her eyes, to keep it. Dress With Trees. It stood the way she sat: half-turned, afraid to move.

At the top of the wide Greek steps she stopped for a final look. She had been there two hours.

The time was up.

Two men, Thai or Korean, walked past her, talking in tongues and moving fast, not wanting to loiter by a woman alone.

She did not go to McAvoy's but caught a cab directly to the sun place. She saw the brown and buff car as they turned down the wide boulevard by the cypress trees. "This is fine," she said, getting out and paying the driver. "I wanted to see the water at sunset."

He figured something was going on, but he didn't want to get into trouble hanging around, so he sped off to catch another fare.

Max's face looked very bad. White and bad. She put the empty gin bottle under the seat. He had taped a note to the windshield: ATTENTION MCAVOY O'HARA.

She could not think what to do, and sat a while in the front seat of the car, watching the swallowing of the sun by the sea. It would not do to be here in the dark. With a dead man.

She got someone to take her to a phone and called an ambulance.

She started to dial Millie, and could not. What if they

had not gone out yet? What was there to say? "What are we supposed to do?" Millie would ask. To which there was no answer.

She thought of the Bitters Road Dump back home.

" *'Song, I am tired to death!'* She said aloud Max's last poem to the beach below. *"Here let me lie where we have paced the moving trees along! . . .'* "

The police came, and emergency medical squads who thought it had been a wreck, and ambulance attendants, and newsmen who thought it was a homicide but when they saw it was Max knew the story and did not write it. They found the bottle. "Dylan Thomas did that," they said, at least a dozen of them. If you were not famous it did not count how you died.

Exhausted, Nell let herself into Millie's house. A note on the counter reminded her they were having dinner with friends.

In the trash the morning paper carried all the news that was fit to print: Diane Keaton bought a fountain pen, Teddy Kennedy visited a child.

She picked up the phone. "Mo," she said, "I'm coming home."

Nick

NICHOLAS HAD COME to San Francisco for a neuro-chemical conference. The papers presented had dealt with how depression, schizophrenia, and what ails you were amenable to psychopharmacology; with the fractionation of DA and NE in small brain samples; with cation exchange resins in catecholamine analyses; with electrochemical detectors in chromatography; and (his own paper) with how birth traumas dominate for life the structuralization of the neuronal arrangement.

His energy was at a low ebb. Conferences were all the same. San Francisco could as well have been Topeka. He had presented a case no one was interested in hearing. The hotel, which rose glass and steel by a park that no one went outside to see, might have been anywhere.

He had come with a sense of anticipation that he would get some feel of the Orient, of Russian and Chinese influence; but had found himself, as in Kansas, in a wholly Western world.

Last night's final banquet address had summed up the substance of the conference: we can drug the world into health again. It was the *again* that bothered Nicholas. The brain could not be where it had never been; he believed that. It fit with the studies that were horrifying everyone, which concluded that the way a child was when he entered school was the way he was when he exited school. School itself, a dozen years of it, caused no difference; it was a mirror that reflected early environment. Educators had been saying for years to the tongue-tied and poor: We can teach your child to be brilliant *again*. The real need was to work on the beginning. To get it right the first time. But he was out of fashion.

He wanted to get out into the city with its immigrants from over the ocean; he thought fondly of Cleveland, whose Poles and Czechs had jammed the St. Lawrence freeway to make a life with talking birds and poodle handbags.

He must have Virginia on his mind. She was full of the outrage engendered by a book called *The Dialectic of Sex*, whose message was that the sexual privatization of women rendered them invisible as individuals to the male eye. "Like any lower class," she would tell him, "our awareness has been deadened."

Something in her rhetoric reminded him of his college days when he had thought himself a radical, but when he had been, in fact, docile and credulous, believing any or all of Darwin, Marx, Freud, because they were apostles, and because his ancestors had not understood them. Now that he passed for a mild-mannered, apolitical man of science, he found he did a lot more real thinking about the supposed predestinations of Random Choice, Class, and Infant Sexuality than he had done in school.

The point was that he did not argue with Virginia's dialectic, but with the fact that it bore no relation to her behavior. Which had not changed.

Outside at dusk, tired of all party lines, he walked down

into the small park adjacent to the hotel. At its four corners street lights illuminated concrete tables set under concrete awnings. At one, to his left, a group of men played a game. The board was painted on the table; the pieces were stones. There were two players and four bystanders, dressed in black cloth suits and close-fitting black hats. They were so small (none could have been more than five feet), that he looked to see if they were boys dressed up. But the lined faces showed not. He did not know if they played Go or Mah-Jongg, having only heard of each, but having played neither.

The game held their attention. It was no casual matter; the bystanders gambled on it.

He sat on a park bench, legs out straight, and watched them. A half level down below (there was the suggestion of terracing the small space, although it was only an apron around the park down half a flight of stairs) he could see a group of boys doing karate or one of the martial arts. They had on satin pants with white sashes and kicked the air like ballet dancers.

He liked the limited concrete world of separate intensities. After a time he crossed the park and entered a Maoist book store, open all night. The interior, which was single-mindedly political, took him back to school days. Posters read:

WHEN THE SERFS STOOD UP IN TIBET

POLITICAL POWER GROWS OUT OF THE BARREL OF A GUN

He thumbed a copy of illustrated acupuncture: *The Yellow Emperor's Classic of Internal Medicine.* A full page showed "the sunlight vessels of the great intestines." Another, "the three burning spaces." Yang and Yin were explained: sweet versus rotten, fragrant versus pungent, song versus grief.

He read a paragraph on the Development of the Woman: At the age of seven her teeth and hair grow longer; at fourteen she begins to menstruate and bear children; at twenty-one she is fully grown and her physical condition is at its best; at twenty-eight her muscles are firm; at thirty-five her face begins to wrinkle and her hair to fall; at forty-two her arteries begin to harden and her hair turns white . . .

Not a book to take a thirty-eight-year-old woman full of anger at her condition as a female. He settled instead on a booklet called *New Women in China*. A woman on the cover swung high above a flock of birds, working in overalls on girders spanning the sky. Inside, women of the Tungling Red Star iron mine consulted on "new ways to exploit the mine." It appeared that women, like men, were now empowered to ravage the earth. (That had to be a Western influence, the man versus woman battle. What had happened to WHEN THE SERFS STOOD UP IN TIBET? Had workers versus owner been forgotten? Here, in the very Maoist bookstore that ought to have protested it, the rubric of liberation divided those who should have been united.)

He debated *New Women*. Would the gesture please her, or would the sight of the coarse-weave coveralls and cropped hair seem to prove her point?

"Hello." A woman spoke beside him.

He saw that she wore a sort of military looking suit that fit their surroundings, belted in a slightly battle-dress style. He saw, also, that she was quite attractive and seemed to know him.

"Hello," he said back.

"I followed you over. You appeared to be by yourself and it was either hope you would go to supper or join the crowds in the bar."

"You're with the conference?"

"I gave a paper this morning."

He was embarrassed. "I'm afraid I was preparing my own."

"I'll tell you about it." She smiled, but did sketch for him her work with schizophrenics. She was British, she said, originally, though not for several years. That partly explained her dress and manner.

He gestured to the shop. "I was something of a Marxist in school—"

"Who wasn't?"

"Over here, not many."

"Then it was important to you?"

"—part of a time that was important."

"I'm not rushing you. I'll look around."

"No, I'm through. I'll get these books." He showed her the sunlight vessels of the great intestine.

Out on the street she said, "I hate conventions. The work seems such a small part of it."

"Why do you come?"

"It looks good on my résumé to present a paper."

She had taught at Princeton, was now at Stanford. He wanted to ask her why she had selected him, but hesitated. He was pleased.

Her name was Margaret Ormandy, and he recognized the name. She had a husband back in England, but "there has been no need to live together for quite some time." No, she had no children.

He talked to her, as they bypassed the hotel and started down the steep hill to Chinatown, of his feeling that the entire west coast belonged to Asia.

She said she had always imagined it Spanish: Balboa peering out at the Pacific on this shore, as, simultaneously, some other Castilian in Siberia claimed it for the king.

"Whenever I hear Spanish spoken, when I'm down in Baja, it makes sense to me. I feel they are the ones who own the ocean."

"Who owns the Atlantic?"

"Why, we do, of course." She smiled widely, showing a broken front tooth, which softened her look and made him feel easier with her.

They talked about New York, and Chicago. She had been disappointed in both. He told her about Cleveland.

"How can it be on the water? It's an inland city."

"The water reaches in."

They talked about the Great Lakes and inland water as opposed to tide waters, seas and oceans.

It was easy. Neither knew a great deal, or had much invested in it. They were quoting school-day information, compartmentalized from never having been used. If your work was such as theirs, they decided, you fell short on general knowledge.

She liked her work, believing that in time schizophrenia would belong in the same archaic category as smallpox or the plague: something for which a cure existed, which could be epidemic if left unchecked, which was influenced by living in groups, but which remained an essentially in-dividual disease, and curable.

Did he agree with that? He wasn't sure. On some level he could be as persuaded that schizophrenia was caused by rats; and bubonic plague by ambiguities within the home. *Cause* was not a simple matter. You had to know where to draw the line.

Chinatown was loud, crowded, filled with people from Chicago and Cleveland and New York buying souvenirs. It was also filled with tea shops and beaded curtains. Nich-olas was constrained from buying anything because he did not want to discuss Virginia. Margaret Ormandy, also, for her own reasons. (Perhaps she did not like to pay for trinkets? Or living in California she might have had her fill of pseudo-culture.)

"Why did you stay over tonight?" he asked her, remembering that she was close to home.

"Once you're back, there is too much to do. When I'm away I don't expect myself to perform. I get angered at these conferences about how little attention is paid to women, but on the whole they are a vacation. I listen with half an ear for anything new, but most of it I have already read, or heard about. The rest of the time I'm freed from deadlines and worry."

"It sounds as if you put pressure on yourself."

"Did you watch the Olympics this last summer?"

"A few times with my daughters."

"When the girl from Rumania, Nadia Comaneci, performed, I found it almost unbearable to watch. The first perfect score in Olympic history, and she got one every time. I know that I will never attain that excellence."

They ate at a Szechuan restaurant. She had hot shrimp with walnuts; he, a mild chicken dish with snow peas. It seemed quite intimate eating out with a woman.

Margaret had her jacket off, showing a filmy tan blouse the same color as the suit. She looked softer, less military, without the jacket, although part of that might have been their being out of the Maoist shop, or his being more at ease with her.

He smiled and decided to deal with where he was. "This is very different for me. I have been married so long that I feel people are watching us."

She did not seem bothered. "I figured you for someone trustworthy; that's why I suggested supper. One feels the need to talk when it is over, but it is easy to be misunderstood."

He was sorry he had spoken. He did not wish to be construed as having said he was not interested in her; rather that he was, but that it felt quite strange and unfamiliar. He could not think what to say now. Perhaps it would be good to let it go, and then, on the way back, stop for a drink, somewhere away from the hotel and common acquaintances.

He felt comfortable and ate a lot. The absence of tension accompanying food was quite rare.

"I'm glad you thought of this," he said.

"Did you know Balboa was beheaded?" she asked. "For all his trouble?"

He was silent.

"That came to me, thinking about the Pacific." She shifted easily in her chair. "I felt you would not mind being approached," she said.

"I have not been on a trip without my wife before, not since we were married eighteen years ago. I think I was waiting for a feeling of relief, or, more importantly, decision, and have encountered only fatigue." He frowned at himself. What a stupid thing to say.

"I understand. Rather than drag it out with my husband for years of recrimination, and bitterness between the families, I have stayed legally married. That, too, makes a kind of fatigue, as you say."

His fortune read: *You will encounter good news.* Hers: *People applaud your good disposition.* They laughed. Fortunes were always so much less than what you wanted. To break the brittle crescent cookie and decipher the tiny print was to be reminded of the height of your expectations.

They stopped for a drink in a small bar with lanterns

and red light and overstuffed seating. It felt as if it had been designed for intrigue, which made it harder to know how to proceed. He wanted to put a hand on her arm, some easy gesture that would alter the dynamics. But he did not.

She began to talk generally about her work and her life. About the backbiting and fights in her department. She seemed, in putting back on her jacket, to have put back on the military quality of her dress.

As they walked along the outer edge of the dark park across from the gambling men in black suits, up the hotel steps, she said, "Nicholas, I feel somewhat awkward with this. I don't want to have created a wrong impression. You looked as if you would be someone it would be good to talk to. I—" She hesitated. "I don't like men very much in that way, in bed. It isn't you. I would not like to have you feel you were not attractive—?" She made it a question, asking for reassurance.

"Not at all," he lied. "I was lonely and my mind is too full of unresolved feelings to be able to offer much anyway."

"Fine, then." She touch·d his arm and buckled her jacket. "It gets chilly when the wind blows."

Instead of riding up with her, which would have been awkward, Nicholas said goodnight by the elevator. He felt let down and at a loss what to do.

He went into the bar. He felt that he had failed. He wanted to pick someone up. Anyone. He wanted to sleep with a woman other than Virginia—a woman who wanted him and thought he would do.

He looked around the small red space. He got a drink to let his eyes adjust to the dim light. This was a five-star hotel; there must be five-star lonely women about.

He embarrassed himself at the thought. He had another

134

drink. The waitress bent over him and let him see down her peasant blouse, but it was all in the line of duty.

After about half an hour, a man and two women came into the dim Chinese-red interior. They appeared to have had a lot to drink already. The women were dressed as if for a cocktail party, in fancy dresses, lots of makeup and jewelry. They both had on dark hose, and under the table their skirts were hiked up to their thighs. They smoked continuously. They were not so much pretty as seductive. The man was quite conventional looking, or, rather, convention-looking.

Nicholas got up—his nerve and to his feet. "May I join you?"

"Sure," the man said. "I can't hog it all."

The women laughed.

One of them seemed familiar to Nicholas, and he sat by her. The familiarity was strong, but he could not place it. It made her easier to consider. She was about thirty-five, and kept swinging her foot under the table, sometimes brushing his ankle. "I'm Edna," she said. "This is Ruth, and this is Clive."

He shook their hands. "I'm here for a convention," he explained, not mentioning what it was, for fear of scaring them off. He gave his name as Nick.

"Aren't we all?" The man spoke. "Why else would you be staying at a fancy place like this? Who could pay?" He leaned back.

"What kind?" The woman, Edna, asked.

"Scientific hardware." Nicholas pulled that out of a hat, pleased with its computer sound.

"We're business communicators," she said proudly.

"Well." He looked for the waitress. This was going to take another drink. "Where are you from?"

"Ruth and I are from San Diego. Clive's from L.A. He says." She laughed. "How about yourself?"

"Cleveland." He did not know why he was lying about his work, or his home. He felt that it was true what he told the trio: that the man sitting here was Nick, from Cleveland, and into scientific props. The kind of man who could pick up a woman in a bar.

Clive told a joke. The women laughed loudly, and Edna looked to Nick for his response.

The way she faced Clive, so that she almost had to turn and look over her shoulder at Nicholas, in the process stretching her dress across her breasts, sent a shock of recognition through him. That and the way the mouth, unexpectedly, turned down when she smiled. It was as if Virginia sat beside him.

Was he setting out, then, to prove that he could be the one she picked up for a change? He started to excuse himself, and then decided, no. He would see, if he were on the other end, what it was like, what the transaction was when it happened this way. Edna looked at him, her face turned to him, her body turned away. He laid a hand on her leg.

"You wear a ring for protection?" Clive pointed to the gold band. "You don't see one on my finger."

"All men are married anyway." The woman named Ruth shrugged.

"Sure we are." Clive patted her shoulder.

They were soon gone, leaving him with Edna, who waited beside him for some action.

He had often thought of the contrast between himself and Virginia. It seemed to him sometimes that something had gone wrong in her brain, something that received signals. It was as if making love made no imprint, so that she never had a sense of having done it, so must repeat it over and over. He felt when he had sex with Virginia that immediately afterward she wanted to be desired and aroused as if nothing had happened, being no more satisfied than before. As if she sat down to breakfast a dozen times in one morning, not having a sensation of having done so only moments before. He, on the other hand, was the reverse. He often felt as if something had already taken place, that the satisfaction or disappointment occured in advance of fact, so that the event itself was, in this sense, secondary. In the case of the woman here in the bar, made up and awaiting his signal, it felt as if they had already gone upstairs, done the act, had the regret and awkwardness. It was as if he had embarked on the job of disentangling himself from her before he had been with her.

He reached for his wallet to pay, to settle the bar bill, having been left with Clive's as well, and found the wallet gone.

"I've lost it—" He felt sudden anger at this last mishap.

"What is this?" Edna stood on her dark legs. She couldn't figure the angle. Was he about to try to stick her with the check? "Look, I don't know what is going on here—"

Nicholas went to the bar and talked to the waitress. "Can I put the tab on my room? My wallet—"

She giggled and the bartender behind her grinned. "Not again," he said.

The girl went around the cash register and handed his wallet to Nicholas. "You look too nice to sweat it out any more."

"I don't get it."

"Oh, Clive does this all the time—the man you were sitting with over there. He gets a big gas out of lifting billfolds. One time, when a guy was really drunk, he took his wristwatch off, and can you believe this, his shoelaces out. He leaves them with me. Then the guys make a big fuss and we all have a big time."

"What do you get out of it?" Nicholas laid down a twenty.

"He leaves a tip, you know, for my part."

The woman, Edna, laughed as if she had not been worried, but it was clear that she had not been in on the routine. Nicholas looked at her and wondered how to proceed.

"I don't go around picking up people," she said defensively, reading his face.

"I don't either. You remind me of my wife. Cleveland is a long way away."

"Sure. I understand." She put an arm through his. "I didn't think you were a hustler."

"I have some Scotch in my room," he said. He wanted to reconsider, to delay, but he knew you could not go back there *again* if you hadn't been there the first time.

"That sounds good to me."

He wanted her; or wanted very much to have done it, which he hoped would pass for the same thing.

She was quite relaxed and began to undress herself and touch him as soon as the door shut behind them. "Do you like this?" she asked as she reached her hands into his trousers. She did not seem to be uneasy about undressing before a stranger. Maybe no one seemed a stranger to her.

He responded to the sight of her breasts, which were larger than he had ever seen and had dark huge nipples that he had not seen even in magazines. That excited him. It was a secret he had access to. When she took off her black underpants he saw that her pubic hair had been shaved into what must have been intended as a heart design. He wondered if that electrified her husband; if he went into rages imagining other men touching it. Nicholas touched her hair and she spread her legs wide and put her own hand there too.

When she pulled him on top she thrust her legs straight up. "Most men like this," she said, rocking back and forth, her legs bucking in the air. "I can keep them up all night," she said proudly. "As long as you want."

She felt hot inside and that was a shock to him. Inside her mouth was hot also, almost scalding. He did not know what made it like that or if he liked it. She began to rock harder and he found he did like the newness of it: the heat, the shaved heart, her pride in what she could do.

After he came, she rolled him off and said: "You can eat me. I don't get that at home. I'm getting to like it."

He put his face down in the clipped hair and did his best. How good that was he could not tell. After a time she unwrapped her big legs from around his neck, and said, "I want a cigarette."

"Why don't you get that at home?" he asked.

"I get all I get during the ball-game commercials." The ruddy woman laughed. "My husband is the fastest man in San Diego."

"Why do you stay with him?"

She had pulled on her panties and bra and was lying on her back. He wanted to see her breasts again.

"Oh, I don't see him that much. I have my job. I have an exercise class one night a week, and a business and professional meeting another. It gets me away. I usually manage to be gone three nights a week. I don't need to work; we have a nice standard of living. I hate his friends; I work with exciting people. It's good enough."

He tried to follow. She seemed to be saying conflicting things: that she was dissatisfied, and that she liked the status quo.

139

She continued. "He doesn't want me to have to work, but as long as I don't need to he doesn't mind. He's proud of my job. I give him something to brag about. Not only in that regard—I think he likes it that other men are attracted to me."

"You don't want out sometimes? Have this all the time?"

"No." She looked uninterested in the idea. "I'd be a fool to rock the boat for a little excitement in my life. When I get plenty anyway."

"How would he feel about this?"

"I do a lot of stuff he hasn't got the balls for. What's the matter? You feeling guilty, Nick? Didn't you like it? She won't mind. What do you think she's doing back home?" She closed her eyes. "Can I get a doze? I'll get up in a little bit; I don't ever stay away all night from my phone."

"I'll take a walk," Nicholas said.

He thought she might be insulted, but apparently she didn't care. She appeared to be asleep at once; it might be that she had had more to drink than he realized.

The walk was a mistake. He had wanted to get out of the hotel room, away from the woman named Edna, but as he went through the late night crowd in the lobby, it seemed to him that everyone was with someone. That at the end of the day's work, people traveled in pairs.

He told himself that most of them were probably at the point where he and Virginia were; he told himself the apparent animation and constant touching were form only. But he did not wholly believe it.

The park was deserted, without even the black-suited serious game-players, or the high-kicking Oriental boys.

He could not go into the all-night bookstore again. Let the sunlight vessels lie.

He had thought things would be better with Virginia

now that Joey and Johnnie, grown into graceful coltish teenagers named Jo and Joni, lived most of their lives preoccupied with boys and at school. He had thought this would free Virginia from the strain of feeling her daughters as constant responsibility, but it had only made things worse.

She felt doubly abandoned, first by Nicholas, now by them. She had taken to calling up her two older sisters again as she had done years ago, trying to reinstate the closeness that they had had as a threesome of girls. He would come home to hear her on long distance to one of them: "It's better but it's just one of those days. Don't worry. My tongue is so sore, it's my sensitivity to what I'm taking. I have so many sensitivities. It's another cluster of blisters coming on the bottom of my mouth. He works all day on those damn rats. One of them died last week, and I won't get half the attention when it's my turn. It has whipped me down."

The girls' growing up had been better for Nicholas. Having stopped taking care of their mother, they had had a little time left over for him. But their strongest tie remained with each other—as, he thought, must always be the case. They seemed as close as he and Richard were, without the animosity; they looked at each other as one looks into a mirror.

This would be their last year at home. His parents, that is, his father, having reconciled himself that there was no one to carry on the Clark name, had acknowledged the future of his granddaughters, and set his mind to their education. Convinced that females especially required a good preparatory school to get into a good university, he agreed to finance their high school years at Exeter.

Nicholas turned in the dark park back toward his room

and its occupant. A sense of fatigue and frustration settled on him like a fog. His own life seemed identical with the conference he had come to attend. In neither did he have an audience for his work; the topic at home, as here, was drugs and not change. San Francisco could have been Topeka. In both, strange men took to bed any woman they could get.

He had not known, until tonight, who the men were who picked up his wife. Now he did: they were him, Nicholas. Nicholas with the splayed feet and flapping ears who had come halfway across the continent to find what he had at home.

He knew that when he returned, he would be back with Virginia *again*.

5

At Home

Nell

———◆———

LAST WEEK TERRY SENT NELL a page cut from an old issue of ARTFORUM, in an article on the partial figure:

> *Consider the powerful conditioning concerned with a fragmented body image to which we are exposed by advertising, medical science, and sports coverage. Daily the mass media mesmerize millions with images of stomach linings, arthritic joints, shattered nerves, aching backs, sluggish bowels, hairless legs, damp armpits, clogged sinuses . . .*

Nell had collected her own fragmented body parts together and explained to Them that Theirs was a common lot. The stomach linings, aching back, sluggish bowels, hairless legs, damp armpits, plugged sinuses, tough scaly elbows propping things up, knees weak with bending to the loss, all responded. (Except mouth, which was not working at the time, out of commission.) They were flattered to be Art. They put on airs for an afternoon: became a torso by Ernst, a pretzeled leg by Giacometti, a cubist arm by Picasso, a knee by Oldenburg. It went to Their head.

Then They settled into comfortable corners and did Their best. Sometimes They got confused—fragmentation was new and painful—and armpits remained dry, face got wet, mind went sluggish, and bowels went loose; legs shattered on the wobbly pebble floor and nerves grew hairless in the north light. But all was allowed. She did not lecture Them. She was gentle while They all recovered.

At first, back in her half-house in San Antonio (Santa Fe abandoned; San Francisco buried where the sea ate the sun), Nell had painted Max's eyes: white, red, lined, blackened, afraid, swollen, haggard, yellowed, open, shut. Now the eyes hung around the room like strings of Christmas lights. Then she did his hands and they now lay folded, knotted, or supplicant, depending on their bent, before the mantlepiece downstairs.

As the separate parts of her body knocked about while she painted pieces of Max (picking at him as if at a sore that would not heal), her internal self took a siesta. Blood did not flow; saliva did not come to the aid of tongue; bowels had locked in protest; throat would not put forth the effort to swallow the situation.

Outsiders had tried to help.

Terry sent this week a review of her San Francisco show:

> *The group show which opened last month at the San Francisco Museum of Art had rather more to it than most such. Several of the artists broke out new works of much more than routine interest. Without the least air of iconoclasm or even self-consciousness, in the group as a whole one saw an ability to make unashamedly personal art. . . . Woodard's curious tonal white-to-white scale, and her immersion in light as form, could not help but call to mind Edward Hopper. One thinks specifically of "Light at Two Lights" (1927) and "Summertime" (1943). . . .*

*From this point of departure, however, Woodard
takes off in an original direction, to present one of
the most compelling, almost minimalistically econom-
ical, collections of the show, at once graceful and
monumentally eloquent.*

"You're our original, darling," voices from the past said
over her disjointed shoulder, reading with her. But they
did not matter: they were from Santa Fe.

Mo was helpful too. She came by with tales from her
welfare work: "I got to the Opportunity Center and this
mother in her third trimester preggers comes up and grabs
me by the butt and shouts so all the kids can hear: 'Keep
an eye on Priestley's pecker for me will you honey it's not
looking so good.' I don't think it looks so good either,
but I don't know what a two-year-old can get. So I keep
an eye on it and at the end of the day he still has it."

When Nell's mouth could not produce words, Mo left,
looking as if she would cry. Only to come again the next
day.

Mommy and Tommy said, "LaNelle, you look like the
wrath of God," and decided to wait this one out.

She grew tired of painting Max's remains. She put out
his eyes and cut off his hands. (They grew lifeless. They
bloated. They smelled. At the end the hands clawed at
themselves like rats. Tore themselves to pieces. The eyes
did not blink.)

She began to paint, then, in earnest. Shirt with Redwoods.
Pollarded Trees with Dress. The shirt tattered and tore,
then billowed and sailed, then shrank and turned tattletale
gray. But she did not let it get away; she nailed it to the

147

tree. Dress tried to turn and run while birds in the top of the stunted trees grew large and mute and malevolent. But she made the Dress get used to it, like the rest of Them.

Mo brought another story from the agency: "Priestley has this bad habit; he kills things. We're modifying his behavior, but gently, so as not to pass judgment on his worth. We are not allowed to say: 'You creep, you killed the goldfish I saw you.' Even his folks make allowances, because he's been in seven foster homes and is Acting Out. So one day the teacher passes around this gerbil, and Priestley squeezes it lifeless. And I say when it's my day: 'Seen any gerbils lately, Priestley?' And he tells me: 'When you squeeze them they want to go to Heaven.' So what am I supposed to do? The gerbil is in heaven, but I'm down here with Priestley."

Mo looked so pleading: Please laugh, her face said.

Nell hunted about for words for those down here below. ("Remedial," elbows whispered. "Cogent," ears offered. "Belated," from the navel. "Equinox," suggested toe. "San Francisco," said the knees, then fell to the floor at what they had done. But they were forgiven; they had supported so much.) "Iced tea?" she blurted out, and with that effort, and the quenching thought, and Mo's relief, recovery began.

She painted rows and rows of little convent dresses for the body parts when They got well. Little gowns, which, in their obedience, did not notice, or were too well-bred to mention, that they were uninhabited. She strung the tiny white dresses like paper dolls about the bed below, like clean laundry hung up to air. Flat as they, she fell to bed exhausted.

Mildew grew on her cheeks, and fungus beneath her eyes; she could not stop the weeping. She blotted, toweled, stuffed hands into sockets, but nothing would stay the

148

flow. Finally she let them pour and painted through them: Shirt with Redwoods, #14. Pollarded Trees with Dress #12.

Maudie Farmer bought one. Mo had hung two or three, to get them out of the way, at the Tea Room. And Maudie had seen the purple and brown shadows in the redwood's trunk, and brought it home, and hung it over her best couch. Now everyone wanted one. "Nell must put them in a gallery," Maudie relayed. "People like that better. It feels more like Art." So Maudie got a Friend to show a selection at her gallery. The rest went to Luciana in Santa Fe.

Nell let Them have time off. She hung up her damp armpits and her stomach linings (which were looking frayed), and her crystal nerves that jangled and chimed at the least sound, and her bowels and joints and sinuses still stuffy (also her breasts, which had dried like raisins without his touch). Even knees, dear knees, got strung up like parts in a puppet show.

It was in the wet season that the dreams began.

The first dream went on for many weeks. Even when she did not dream it she woke remembering she had; and when she did dream it, she woke so fatigued she thought maybe she hadn't. It went like this: She entered a small crowded bathroom with north light, a white guest bath-room, and stood in the shower in the long white Wedding Dress. There, ever so carefully, she severed her wrists, and then, neatly, held her hands to the side, under the cold shower, so as not to spot the dress. When she felt tired, she shut her eyes, leaned back against the tub, wrists turned away, and let the water wash her white as the dress.

That part was soothing: she had done it in a ladylike, orderly manner. No one could fault her. Terry and the

Friends would appreciate the Art of it; Tommy and Mommy, the restraint.

Then, the bad part started. What she had not planned. The tub did not drain. The hem of her dress clogged it. She couldn't move to clear it, tore at it. The tub began to fill and she, who had been moments before dying graciously, began to drown. Choking she woke up, unable to breathe, lungs begging for air. In her sleep or on waking she screamed: "No, no, I didn't mean that."

After the dream, They comforted her. There is no way to die that does not feel wrong, They told her. See, that is a lesson for you. The damp armpits and the clogged sinuses and the hairless legs gathered about as the knees knocked out their message: Don't. They were afraid that she would forget Them in her silent movie in the shower, all They had done for her. I wouldn't do that, she said, not after all we've been through together. I wouldn't do that to You.

The last time she had the dream she worked it out and let it go. The hem caught and the blood stained the bath water pink, but did not drown her. She managed to shut it off in time. Mommy thought she had chosen the pink Christening Dress to depart in, and was touched, as pink was her favorite color. Nell woke laughing and They rattled their bones all night at the sound.

Then the next dream began. She woke from it the first time pulling herself up out of her sleep hand over hand as if she were pulling up by a rope. "Where are we?" she asked Them, climbing out of it. She was at the aunts' house, hunting for toilet paper and finding jams, searching for the eggs and finding cold winding bobbins in the egg crates, needing sugar and sweetening her tea with rat poison, wanting fruit and finding crocus bulbs. Wanting to go home and being locked in the closet with the paper goods that never ran out. Wanting a daddy and rocking back and forth on Tommy. Wanting her Babies Room and having keys only to the Red Room, Blue Room, Rose Room. Searching them all in her lavender gabardine suit (with yellow gloves) for the bone china roses, which were gone.

She did not retrieve them. In time the dream became a shorthand: she stood in the Rose Room and the mantle was blank. The mirror reflected nothing. And then, she dreamed only of the mirror with no reflection.

And then she got about her business.

Limbs began to appear in her pictures. She did a white uniform to resemble the slightly yellowed cheap nylon of old women's hair. It was a size 44, a fatty dress. Big wobbly knees appeared below the dress. Robust knees. She knew where they came from; it was her debt to Them. She would do dozens of trusty uniforms, some with rough elbows, some with chapped hands, some with varicosities. She owed Them a lot.

Pink seeped back into her paints. The light of late summer dusk, fragrant with crepe myrtle: she aimed for that. Whereas in Santa Fe she had fought to keep rose tones out, here she fought to keep them in. The flat Texas light bleached the pinks to faded peach, to creams, to newsprint yellow, to old-book ochre.

She wanted to do an Evening Dress, a first blush dress, with puffed sleeves and tentative open arms. It would have a sweetheart neckline; its hem would dip up to a small bouquet of rosebuds. It would be a dress to break the heart. A dress for all of them who had believed in love.

But something did not go right with it. It hung about in an unhappy state. She could not figure it out, and then, one night, she did. Forgetful of her recent bad times, her hands and eyes had painted, by mistake (no malice intended), the dress of her dream. The one that had drowned in the bathtub, dyed pink from her cut wrists.

She discovered that her shambles were contagious: everyone wanted the same. What she did not understand was why seeing love tear someone's bones loose made everyone else want to try it too. Lemmings to the sea.

Mo's fifteen-year-old twins were going steady. According to their mother, with Abercrombie Fitch and Merrill Lynch.

(It was hard to tell Frank and Stein apart from their grandmother's naming and their mother's reaction to it. She seldom glimpsed their actual selves.)

Alfred began to drop by the half-house, wearing a wretched look. He didn't want to eat, or talk. His cheeks were hollow.

Nell cast about and thought of Terry; he was a Friend. She told her son the art collector was coming by.

"But he's a homosexual."

"Oh, really?" Nell gazed at the seventeen-year-old.

"Dad said."

"That was not his word."

"He and Amaryllis think it's odd that you see him."

"Queer to see a queer." Nell now had two chairs for guests and kept pots of white flowers in the fireplace for summer.

"They don't know about, uh, Max, so they think—" He decided not to pursue that. He remained a good boy, not wanting to give grief to his mother. Wary of her now that she had produced evidence of so much of it on her own.

"But if I am to keep you from homosexual men and heterosexual women, for fear of seduction, then you are safe, it is clear, only with women who love women. But then, that would be a danger to me. Whom can we see?"

"I decided you felt comfortable being with someone you would not fall in love with." His voice was muffled.

She studied him when Terry came. "Alfred says you may not be safe."

Terry smiled and shook the boy's hand. "My dear, I am interested only in elderly pianists with leonine hair. Something like my father. Didn't you read up on all that?"

Terry sat and accepted wine. He looked so young himself, except for the dark circles around his eyes and the lines in his cheeks. His body, his way of moving, looked no older than her callow son. They had on matching tennis shoes.

"Alfred thinks," she said later—after they had talked about the fact that Maudie Farmer had made Nell's name quite chic and that the Plum Line Gallery had sold two dozen variations on Trees with Dress and Shirt—in what she hoped was a casual way to get to the heart of her son's disease, "that it could be nice to be around someone you would feel comfortable not falling in love with."

"He has, we assume, the opposite problem?" Terry crossed his legs and looked at the boy. His air was one of confidentiality but not intrusion.

"This is my guess—" Nell said, as gently as possible, not looking at her son.

"I don't know what you're getting at, Mother." The sandy slender boy had the sound of misery.

They had always been such cowards with one another. Preferring to let it go rather than to deal with it. This seemed the time to break the rule. "Terry, when I first heard of Astilbe, Alfred said she was his girlfriend. Tucker, to his dense discredit, has moved her into Alfred's house, where she now occupies the role of sister. And has for quite a while."

"She's going off to college—" Alfred said, staring down.

"In two years."

"I know—"

Terry leaned toward the boy, his arms resting on the chair. "Do you have a picture of her?"

"Yes." Alfred got out his wallet and there, in the plastic pocket, was a young and lovely face.

Terry got what he must have known by intuition that he would when they saw Alfred look at her.

The boy's eyes had tears in them. "I don't know how you knew, Mother."

"You said it straight out, I thought."

"I didn't mean to."

"What can be done, Terry?"

"It depends." The collector had another glass of wine and studied the painted roses and eggs and wedding dress that he knew by heart. They talked of a show he had seen in New York at the Whitney. As he was leaving, he offered: "Alfred, it would be pleasant if you and your mother came to supper at my house. The backyard is in bloom and my housekeeper does some wonderful things with snails. Bring Astilbe if she's at home this summer. Non-sexual relationships will be the order of the day." He smiled slightly.

Nell walked him out the door. How well he did things. His last note to her in the bad times was tacked above the pebbly floor upstairs, to save for relapses. At his car he said to her, not for youth's ears, "What we need to see, dear, is whether he wants this girl especially or only wants again someone he cannot have."

"My fault?"

"That's the nature of Mother. Don't berate yourself. I

154

could provide someone more suitable, less disastrous. I'll look among my married Friends for someone restless."

She smiled. It was good to have help in time of need.

"Will he say anything?" Alfred sat in his chair, unable to cover his misery.

"No. I trust him. Or I wouldn't have had him come by."

He got up to go, and then asked, "Are you doing all right, Mother?"

"I seem to be, don't I?" She dismissed the question. You did not get all right, you got on with it.

Mo still brought Nell news from the outside world of red-tiled roofs, white caladium, and houses bought and sold in Almost Park. "You wouldn't believe," she said, "what I overheard at the Tea Room. This woman, Maudie's friend, was saying, 'So my husband's father called him into his office, because he had a really grave thing to discuss, and he had his secretary hold all calls, and so my husband thought at least he was changing his will, or had heart cancer or something, and do you know what he said? He said, "Son, your mother and I have talked it over and we have to tell you that those green chairs in your living room don't work . . ." ' "

Nell considered her pretty sister, her hair lighter than in the past, her cheeks brighter. She wasn't sure how she knew, but she did. She thought she must have acquired a gift, the hard way.

"Are you having an affair?" she asked.

"Me? Mother of Eagle Scouts? Preserver of Priestley's pecker?"

They were in the backyard, by the tire swing and the dried patch of yellow grass where once a garage had been. In Nell's coming home some change had taken place in their visiting: they no longer took their coffee in Mo's Mexican kitchen, but instead sat at Nell's half-house, often on the outside stairs. Today they sunned their legs in shorts, drinking their coffee iced.

Nell was going to let the matter go. There were some things you did not have to share.

But Mo seemed relieved. "How could you tell?" she asked, blushing.

"I don't know. I think I recognize the symptoms."

"It must be because we're so close."

"Is this new?" Nell knew she had been recently inattentive.

"It happened while you were falling apart with Max, so, you know, I couldn't very well talk about it then. And for one thing, of all the people in the world I'm the last one to do this, how the hell can I find time, with Frank and Stein and Trey and the Less Fortunate at the Opportunity Center and all the stuff we do? But somehow I am. I've known him forever, which is what makes it so dumb. We're just like brother and sister. I think we're having a teenage crush after all these years of being buddies.

"It's not the thing where you die if the phone doesn't ring and you attack the mailman to see if he has a letter. We agreed not to write or call, but just to meet."

"Do you love him?"

"I guess so. He's wonderful. He's my best friend. I guess I had to try it once. You know?"

Nell nodded her head yes, but she did not know. She did not want some of someone and some of someone else. Fragmentation was easy enough to come by on your own without asking for it. She did not want that which was not necessary; that which you agreed to make less than it was. She thought of Alfred and wondered if Terry might be wrong; it might be that inside his coward's clothes, Alfred burned as his mother had. "Who is it?" she asked.

"I'd better not say. That way, I mean if you don't know then you don't have to play dumb when his name comes up. Please don't say anything; I know you won't. I'd die if Trey even guessed—"

"Just tell me what you want to," Nell said. She could feel the tears return.

"I've upset you. I'm so stupid. Here Max is dead and you don't have anybody and I'm running off at the mouth about having two men. I could bite my tongue off. I mean in one way you never really had anybody, did you? You and Tucker were over so quick and then Max drinking and all like you said. You never really had anything. Not that lasted."

Nell watched Mo, who looked about fifteen in her shorts with her big grin and her hair tied up with a ribbon. She looked so pleased to be playing love affair.

"When will you see him again?" Nell asked.

"In half an hour." Mo giggled. "At that motel near your café."

Of course nothing lasted. Nell knew that. But she also knew that some things did not even start.

When she had lived in the half-house before, a woman alone, you could have set the sun's rising by her order. She woke without a clock; so timed was she that she functioned as her own alarm. She could feel again the tying of her tennis shoes, the firmness of her legs, sense somewhere down the street the impatience of the youthful dogs. Breakfast at the café was biscuits, eggs, lots of coffee. Mornings up the steps outside went to the labor of that first attempt at Wedding Dress. Lunchtime meant clean shirt, clean hair, clean brown pants. In the afternoon a visit at Mo's—or sometimes one here with little Alfred. Evening was the sound of her white room and early to bed. Alone by choice.

Her thinking then had been that if she kept her body healthy, her mind concentrated, her fingers working, her coffee hot, the dogs panting, that it would be Good. Her greatest wish at that time was to be doing all day what she did all day.

That was then.

Now was different. What was she to do? The limp-wristed pink dress had been shoved against the wall. The uniforms went on strike. Arms, legs, knees roused Themselves and suggested biscuits. It was four in the morning.

It was an enormously safe world in the early hours. All the big houses were electrically wired against theft and intrusion; all the smaller ones with the larger trees had police protection. She liked being out.

She went to the café on Broadway. In the depths of the night there were no custody fathers or clerical workers, not even truckers, as the highway had not run through town for years. Only the lonely were there. A few lovers who were parting to go home to account for themselves; those who could not sleep due to splitting heads or ghostly silences. Red and Shred, the two surviving elderly dogs, growled as she went by, deep in dog sleep, thinking her a prowler, and then, recognizing her step, went back to eyeless dreams of chasing cars.

She visited with Vera, the waitress. A woman who also worked the nightshift. "You back here to stay, honey?" Vera asked.

"It looks like it."

"You divorced or what?"

"Divorced and what."

"You want biscuits with those eggs?"

Nell did, and jam, too, and sausage.

"You like this job?" she asked Vera.

"Best I ever had. It gets me out of the house away from the kids and the old man. Gives me a little peace not to mention peace of mind. He can't think I'm up to anything in this place."

Nell considered her own job. Was it the best? Puckering pink dresses on a pebbly floor by night, plucking away at the past by day. She couldn't be sure. It was too soon to tell. Her going and coming seemed a cake that hasn't cooled, gelatin that isn't set, a soufflé that might fall. (It might be better to do something like repair sewing machines; your work would be going well when they all hummed along.)

"Working nights I get to see my kids," Vera said.

"How many do you have?"

"Three."

"That's nice."

"I get to see them in the daytime, not like some working mothers. I'm there when they get home from school so I know they're not getting theirselves in trouble. Not like some mothers. Then I get some peace here at night."

"When do you sleep?"

"I don't need a lot." Vera shrugged. "I sleep mornings. The old man gets their breakfast."

"Sounds all right."

"It's the best job I ever had."

Nell considered it as she walked home through the close, quiet neighborhood. (Dog echoes came from the backyards as she went by.)

That night in the white bed she gathered Them around her. "It's too vicarious," she said, "—other people." They said: "We told you so." "I want one of my own," she said. "A life." They knew she would come around. There was cheering and hugging and crying as They piled into bed with her and the lot of Them settled down to a good night's sleep.

Nick

H E H A D W A I T E D S O L O N G for this afternoon that it seemed to have already happened long ago. A fear that he was never in the present moment surfaced. He reassured himself: the only present is the past. He walked under the tall trees at the Menninger Clinic toward a meeting room whose occupants awaited him.

"This job does not mean nor is intended to suggest the necessity for a career change," Dr. McCall, head of the Fellows Program, had told him a fortnight ago in making him the official offer to become a member of the interdisciplinary team of Research Fellows at the psychiatric clinic.

The opportunity, which he had accepted eagerly, would provide him with grant funds, a laboratory, and, above all, at last, unearmarked time to work exclusively on his attempt to prove that the initial chemistry of the brain at conception was, in some manner, passed on genetically.

"I will remind you, however," Dr. McCall had continued, "that your predecessor, as I'm sure you know, came to us also a neurochemist, having done fine work in left and right neurotransmitters and their possible role in psychopathology, and left us, as you may not know, to become a clinical psychiatrist. I have to warn you, there's something in the atmosphere that's catching."

They talked in the clinic cafeteria over a lunch of scrambled eggs, cottage cheese, green beans, and pudding, whose calorie counts were posted on signs above the buffet line. The dining room served both staff and patients—the latter distinguishable by the fact that they were clearly wealthier. McCall finished his plate and leaned closer. "I'll be frank, Nicholas, the reason you were chosen had more to do with a man who is dead than with any of us doing the selecting."

"How is that, sir?"

"You remember Edward Cavender?"

"I thought a great deal of him."

"Apparently he returned the sentiment. Before he died— you may recall that it was not sudden, as he had time to set his things in order, too much time many of us thought, I for one, he himself, I suspect, for another—at any rate, he said to me that he wanted to settle the matter of your coming to the clinic. We had your predecessor here at the time, had recently taken him on in fact, but nonetheless, Edward impressed upon me that it was his wish, and would not cease to be his wish even though he was not here to enjoin me concerning it, that you be taken on as part of the team. I agreed, mainly, I confess, to put his mind at ease—not being familiar with your work at the time—as there was no way to render that service for his body, regrettably. I promised to do what was in my power. As you see, I succeeded."

"I am grateful, sir. To you as well as to him. I had no idea—" Nicholas was sure that McCall had had to fight over some opposition to get another neurochemist named to the team, when psychologists and psychohistorians were standing in line. He had tried to convey his thanks.

* * *

The Cavenders seemed always to be there for him when he needed them most. He remembered again the visit he had made to them, a schoolboy, the summer before college. And another, more important call, that he had paid four years later when forced to make a final choice of a field of work.

He had vacillated during his undergraduate years between two paths, that of history and that of science. None of his classmates had understood. To them, the fields were disciplines apart. That was the problem: the use of such words as *field* or *discipline*. If you did not think in those terms, but looked at mankind, there seemed no point at which to decide where the past of a thing (its history) ceased, and its nature (science) began. For Nicholas, every event or object permitted at the same time both ways of considering it.

He had mentioned this to his father. But received in reply only a concern that his son achieve success as he understood it.

"Stay at Harvard," his father had urged. "With your grades and record, your family connections—"

"I'm not sure I want to."

"We live in an academic age. Without the prestige of a top university, you have no forum. I know."

"I'll see. If I go into research, I might stay in Kansas."

"We have such high hopes for you."

"I know, Dad."

He had reached a point his senior year—for he believed that decisions were made long in advance of consciousness —of thinking that he must already know what he wanted to do if he could only become aware of that knowledge. A sentence from his undergraduate reading came back to him, from Sartre's *Nausea: "The thing is that I rarely think; a crowd of small metamorphoses accumulate in me without my noticing it, and then, one fine day, a veritable revolution takes place.*"

His belief was (and it was in fact a *belief* in the sense of an enormous, perhaps a foolish, faith) that Dr. Cavender and his wife could tell him what it was he had decided to do.

"Well, Nicholas," Dr. Cavender had greeted him warmly.

"You've come to report to us on school as you promised. How nice." Mrs. Cavender seemed older, plumper, grayer —but as kindly as he remembered. He sat with her more comfortably this time, waiting for cake and coffee and the measuring cup of brandy.

"I want to hear all about it," she pressed.

He felt awkward beginning without Dr. Cavender in the room, but he talked falteringly about his indecision between history and science. Put that way, he felt a fool, as if he were asking her to give him graduate course advice.

"It's good of you to drop in on us," the psychiatrist said when he carried in a tray of coffee and store-bought brownies, which he explained he always jazzed up with a melted Hershey bar on top.

"Sir, you see—" Nicholas had stumbled over his words.

Mrs. Cavender came to his rescue. "He is trying to decide between history and science, Edward."

"Oh, my." The man looked at his wife and smiled. "Imagine that."

She looked back at him fondly. Then, to Nicholas: "You see, we wrestled with that dilemma too."

"Or so we saw it at the time," Dr. Cavender continued. "Maisie was in history when we met; and I, in physics. But the more she saw of the experimental method and the more

164

I saw of how a thing was explained by its past, well, some-how we got changed around; she went into microbiology, a connection you might not at once perceive, and I, into psychotherapy. At any rate, as you have seen, there is no way to separate the two. Anything you go into, if you do it right, is part and parcel history. But when you winnow out your reactions to it, then it is science."

Nicholas felt overwhelmed. Here was what he had been thinking, put into better words by people who had them-selves gone through the same decision. He could hardly believe his ears. He felt close to tears at the enormity of not only being understood, as he had never been anywhere, but at being previewed, and by better, more serious minds. "I didn't think anyone else—" he tried to tell them.

"But we do," Mrs. Cavender reassured him. "It is the place one gets to if one goes deep enough."

"It is? Everyone?"

"I think so, don't you, Edward?"

"If we can help you, Nicholas. We found that in the end it came down to this: which would you rather spend your time on day by day, or, rather, day by day, which do you find that you already spend time on?"

"What am I actually doing?" Nicholas asked it aloud; not of the Cavenders, but of himself. It was the first time he had had the concept, although it would be several years before he had the words, of *look at the behavior*. "I think I want to see where a thing is going—"

"Well, then," Dr. Cavender said. "So did Maisie." He looked again tenderly at his wife. "We always take our nap when she gets home—"

When Nicholas rose, Mrs. Cavender stood and hugged his chest. "You'll be fine," she said.

He had an urge to pat the top of her head.

*   *   *

That was almost nineteen years ago and he never went back. It had not occurred to him to do so. He had got their revelation; and their blessing. It would have felt presumptuous to return. He had not even called on Mrs. Cavender when he learned that Dr. Cavender had died; sure that she would not remember that muddled boy.

What a lonesome time she must have had of it these last four years—napping by herself.

Remembering that conversation with the Cavenders made him think of the French molecular biologist, Nobelist Jacques Monod who, Nicholas had read, had, at the end— dying of leukemia but not yet aware of it—decided to make a change and write a book on man and time instead of molecules and time: To make the move from science to history. "And why not?" he was supposed to have asked, over a bowl of fruit on a French afternoon.

Nicholas had not agreed with Monod's scientific conclusion that man was no more than "an anxious quest in a frozen universe"; but he had had a deep response to Monod's historical concept that the need for a complete explanation of things was inborn, and that the absence of knowing man's assigned place in the universe begot "a profound ache within." It was this ache that seized Nicholas whenever he went to the lab.

His mind shifted to the work he had chosen. Monod, who insisted that there was only chance behind the grand design of mankind, had had to acknowledge Lamarck's attempt to explain the close interconnection of anatomical adaptations and specific performance; to concede that there appeared to be some response to need in the universe, at the least a shift in behavior that made selection more favorable.

166

What shift, and how, was the question Nicholas' new job would give him the time to answer.

The other Fellows awaited him in the conference room: two women, young and serious; four men, not so young or so serious. The women were in literature and psychohistory; the men in philosophy, human development, sociology, and theology. Dr. McCall, a distinguished white-haired gentleman, had coffee for them, and sharpened pencils and pads. Nicholas was the only new member, so the briefing had very much the air of an inside club.

A television camera came into view, and two reporters with it. This session was being televised, as Dr. Nicholas Clark's entrance into the group was an excuse for valuable publicity on team work at the clinic. Nicholas felt himself tense, and then relax. This was a small but essential part of his job; it was his dues.

McCall read the Fellows, for their consideration, from a paper on "Affects in Borderline Disorders": " 'Very often borderline patients exhibit basic moods which predispose them to certain emotional reactions later in life—anxiety, anger, boredom. Especially boredom in this sense, as for the borderline patient it becomes a prolonged affair. It is characterized by a sense of longing for something (or someone) that is not merely absent but nonexistent, or at best undefinable, something that leaves one feeling empty or hungry, "hopeful" in a very hopeless way.' "

How did the team feel about that? How could each of their specialties touch on such a person? Borderline work was new and necessary. McCall quoted Dr. William Menninger: " 'There are many people in the world who are neither our patients nor our students, and who are nonethe-

167

less filled with great apprehensiveness . . .' "

(Nicholas was struck with how the words seemed to describe Virginia.)

The psychohistorian discussed her study of the transmission of values; the theologian tied in Teilhard de Chardin with Freud; the sociologist discussed language specimens of disturbed individuals; the philosopher spoke on ethics. Nicholas, when it was his turn, talked of beginnings. He ended with a quote from his predecessor, to pay his public tribute: " 'In man, combinations of genetic inheritance and the somewhat existential vagaries of nature, such as birth traumas and early postnatal influences, tend to dominate the structuralization of the neuronal arrangements. It matters very much how these are put together. The hard wiring is relatively fixed, but how the systems interact to produce the ultimate mental activity is open to modulation. We can say that this chemistry is the neurophysical counterpart of developmental psychiatry.' "

A reporter asked Dr. McCall a question, to which he answered, "No, no, I think not, not in that sense. They do not all deal with behavior; we are not reductionists."

Then, back on camera, Dr. McCall, beaming beneath his white mustache, gave a summary, as if to the Fellows, in fact to the video audience, on the interrelation of the sciences and mental health, a cross-fertilization process that brought new minds and new disciplines to solve old problems.

The camera and the rhetoric disappeared.

"We did this same thing last year, Oscar," the psychologist said to McCall.

"It never hurts. It never hurts to have good will. Private institutions are not endowed with that." He made a joke that sounded as if it had been made before. "Let's get lunch,

168

shall we?" McCall took Nicholas' arm. "We've earned it, I'd say."

In the last year, Nicholas' parents had initiated high tea. His mother had found an antique silver samovar, so that tea had taken on overtones not only of the British, but also of the Russian. At least she told that to company, with the implication that in both countries the serving of tea connoted nobility.

Frank now took Wednesday afternoons off from his practice, in order that they might invite, to the cool dim high-ceilinged library, a visiting celebrity or old friend to come by, for a sampling of Mary Ann Clark's charm, and her husband's educated curiosity.

Virginia did not go with Nicholas.

"Next they'll be wanting you to arrive in short pants, so they can tell the story about brilliant Nickie asking How does he know he's not walking around sound asleep. Well, there is no way I'll do that scene. You don't see Richard dropping by for high tea with his naked forest ranger, now do you?"

Nicholas went, when he could, on Wednesday afternoons alone.

This afternoon the coffee table held open-faced cucumber sandwiches with watercress and, beside them, frosted petits fours. A midsummer repast that seemed intended to welcome.

Yet the atmosphere in the room denied it. He looked at his parents, and then saw that they had company.

On the small couch sat an old woman who looked like a peasant. She had thick legs, worn-down brown shoes, her hair pinned back in a knot from which wisps strayed carelessly. He could not see her face—but he recognized her at once. It was Mrs. Cavender.

With surprise and pleasure he went forward and took her hand.

"This is Nicholas, my firstborn, whom I don't believe, of course, I was, for that matter, a firstborn, too, of my father, although not my mother who was not you see—" His mother almost whispered in the highly charged atmosphere.

"Nicholas," his father took over, "this is Dr. Maisie Cavender. You may have known her late husband at the clinic in some capacity. She has come to call on us, which puts us to shame, as we failed to pay our respects when she lost her husband." His father seemed stiff, as if he were holding himself in with great effort.

"Hello, Nicholas." The round straggly woman smiled at him. "It's been too long."

"It has. And that's my fault. I was thinking about you and your husband on the way over here, Mrs. Cavender." He sat down beside her.

"I didn't know, you knew . . . ?" His mother fluttered her hands.

Remembering how Dr. Cavender had brought his wife cake and coffee, Nicholas piled a plate high with cucumber sandwiches and frosted pastries for her.

"She didn't really come, you see, she just stopped by, I'm sure, it's almost time for dinner, we have usually . . ." His mother protested the offering.

Mrs. Cavender addressed Nicholas: "Actually, I came to congratulate you; and realized that naturally this was no longer your home. In the old days I would have called your number and made a proper appointment. But now my eyes are not what they should be. I cannot see at night, nor in broad daylight, so I have to make my way along in the twilight times. On foot, as I can no longer drive a car.

Sometimes I think I've outlived myself, but then, I'd like to see how it all turns out." She took a bite of sandwich eagerly. "Edward and I used always to nap at this time, so, foolish old woman that I am, I do my errands then. When I realized my mistake, I had intended simply to leave my card for you with your parents. That is how I happen to be an uninvited guest for this tea party."

"But it is a pleasure," Nicholas said. "I came from the clinic."

"Yes, I know. Oscar McCall telephoned me. I wanted to go, to represent Edward, but I am not able. My eyes are not what they should be."

"The clinic?" Nicholas' father frowned.

He reminded his father that today was the formal announcement of the interdisciplinary appointment.

"Certainly. I had temporarily forgotten. I assume it went as expected?" His tone was cool.

"Edward would have been quite pleased—" Mrs. Cavender said.

"My own father was known, of course, for his work, at one time, throughout Kansas, the one man, not that he limited himself to hybrid wheat, his work was often . . ." Mary Ann pressed her hands together.

"—I owe a debt to him," Nicholas replied to their guest.

The old woman got up from the couch, rising laboriously. She licked her lips slightly from the food. To Nicholas she said: "Now that I have been fortunate enough to pay my respects in person, a happy event, I think I should be on my way. I can't function as I would like after dark with these eyes of mine." She turned to his parents: "Do forgive my arriving unannounced."

Nicholas walked her out onto the sidewalk, as she would not accept a ride. She was very dear to him. He patted her head, as he had wanted to long years before.

"You'll be all right," he told her.

"I expect so." She thanked him. "They are angry with you, I perceive. One day it might benefit us to have a further talk. Go back in now and see to it. Goodnight, my dear, and congratulations." She was gone, moving slowly down the street.

His mother was stretched out on the small couch. The scene brought back the one years ago, with his mother in a swoon from the dog smoldering on the sidewalk.

His father was comforting her: "Dear heart, I have never been more proud of you. Such poise and presence in front of that intruder. In the face of what you have been through today—"

"What is it, Mother?" Nicholas stood in the doorway. He hesitated to enter the atmosphere of the room.

His father straightened, speaking with effort. "How could you walk in our house in this manner, as if nothing had happened?"

"He never, even as a child, you remember, no one came, his birthday party, he was always, an isolated, I can't blame, a mother can only—" She gasped for breath.

"I am in the dark."

"Virginia, your wife, she told us, all the words you used, coarse, to a woman, she said, such vile language, not even, my firstborn—"

Frank made it clear. "Your wife came to us this afternoon with the news that you had summarily thrown her out of your house, that now that your daughters were old enough to board off at school she was not needed any more. She stated that you had not wanted her as a wife for some years, and that you had been explicit—and she quoted, I will tell you, your exact language—in your wish to be rid of her. We, naturally, offered her a temporary refuge here, but she said she had contacted your brother Richard, who had agreed that she should stay with him until she had recovered herself sufficiently from the shock to look for residence and employment. She was, understandably, too upset to consider any future plans at this time. We understood she had had no more warning than we in this matter."

Nicholas stood frozen. A hard knot inside him seemed to fill his body until he felt set in stone. He could not speak. He tried to simulate in his mind the scene of Virginia's histrionics abutting his mother's hysteria.

"Do you not have anything to say for yourself? Did you not think we would be told of this? Did you think you could cast off your wife and appear at our house for tea as if nothing had occurred?"

The words that came foolishly to Nicholas' mind were: *But you never liked her.* What he said, instead, was: "I have no idea what you are talking about, Father." How could they believe that there could be an innocent reason for his wife moving in with his brother? He saw Virginia as he had left her, in slacks and t-shirt, barefoot, hair uncombed, shouting.

"You deny it?"

"I do," he said.

"I think it would be best if you went. For your mother's sake, if not for your own."

"You're right. I should go home." He turned and left. The stone had disappeared from inside him and left in its place: amazement.

"Well, what the hell did you expect me to tell them? That I was going to Richard's because we'd been fucking for twenty years and I got tired of doing it on the sly, and besides, with the kids going off being preppies, what was the use anyway? And you were never home so you wouldn't even notice? Is that what you would have preferred?"

Virginia had on a dress, her hair was still damp from washing, and her suitcase was packed. She had waited for him to get the news and come home. Richard was to get her at dinner time, after she'd had it out with Nicholas.

"Why didn't you tell me this morning?"

"You wouldn't have heard. You were rehearsing your speech. You had your big meeting on your mind. I could have cut my throat in front of you and you would have stepped over me on your way out the door. What if I said I *did* tell you? You couldn't be sure, could you? Well, I've had enough of nothing. I've got something, now, and I've got news for you, I've had something all along."

"Has it always been Richard?"

"We did it the day you and I got back from our honeymoon." She watched his face.

"I had not considered that."

"What did you think?"

"I don't know."

"Did you think I was picking up anybody who came along? There was never really anyone but Richard, the rest didn't count. He's always been on my side. I could tell him things I could never tell anybody. He doesn't go into permanent shock if people are the way they are. Who else in this buggy clan was I supposed to get any help from? Mary Ann and Frank are deaf and blind to anyone they're not impressing."

"I wish we could have settled this between ourselves."

"There's nothing between ourselves, is the point. I went

174

over there because it is so easy to jam their gears that I thought if they were mad at you they'd never figure the rest out. Not beneath their noses. Not in a hundred years."

He sat on the purple bed. Her suitcase was open on it. She seemed energized by the scene she had created, and moved continually about the room.

"What are you going to tell Jo and Joni?"

"That I walked out. What does it matter what I tell them? They don't care. All they think about is boyfriends. They've got their own lives, they've had enough of mama. I told my sisters and they think all my headaches will go away. They think you're the biggest headache in my life."

Nicholas considered his daughters, and saw this leaving in a new light. He saw their confident, clannish faces, their coltish girls' bodies. He had had so little of them. Was this to be a final alienation? What would they piece together of their mother and their uncle?

"What's the matter? Distracted you to remember you've got kids?"

He saw in her anger a sudden glimpse of what must be true: "Richard wanted you to wait until they were off at school."

"What if he did?" She opened the draperies.

"He wants no strings."

"That's fine with me. I don't want any either. He and I understand each other."

"Does he get to keep his girlfriends?"

She flared up. "They were for show. He didn't care about them. It was always me."

"Why did you marry me?"

"Because he didn't want to."

"You came out here because of him?"

"Don't make yourself sick about it. I thought if I was

around, and he had a chance to see me a lot . . . It wasn't some big plot. I wasn't your property, you know. I wasn't like a car or house or something you bought."

Nicholas had never won a round with Richard, not ever, not once.

He remembered asking himself, as far back as the Mother's Day of the inexplicable *Reader's Digest* article, if he did not secretly wish to give Virginia back to his brother. He had avoided the answer—because even if he had admitted to the fact, he would not have known how. He could never have done this on his own.

Only Richard could have made this happen. Richard gave and Richard took away: their mother, the birthday parties, the dog, Virginia. (And now, that which he wanted more than any of the earlier gifts: his freedom.) The hated link with his brother went back to the beginning.

"I'm not taking much with me—" Virginia said, anxious at his continuing to sit there.

"I want the divorce final by Christmas," he told her. It had come to him suddenly that she might intend the present situation to exist for years: his family on her side; Richard the prairie samaritan taking her in; her making pathetic but ineffectual attempts to get jobs; his still being her legal husband.

If she were single the reason for her living with Richard could not be evaded. His family and his daughters could not be lied to.

"I'm not filing," she said defensively. "You can deal with that mess."

He had been right. "I want it over," he repeated.

"It's over. It's been over. It hasn't ever been there." She looked uncertain.

He didn't respond.

"Richard understands I'm fed up and can't take any more."

Nicholas stood at last. "Does he understand that I am? Tell him that."

He felt a terror that it might be revoked, that she would run after him to the car and say that she had not meant it. That she would patch it up with his family—and it would be as if none of this had ever taken place.

Later, in a motel on the edge of town where he had registered under another name, lest she find him, Nicholas watched himself on the evening news. Sitting among the clinic Fellows he looked a clumsy forty-ish man with ears that stuck out. It was only when he spoke of his work that he became animated.

He had told McCall, "This is one of the happiest days of my life."

He sat on the bed a long time before he noticed that he was crying at the truth of it.

6

Different Places

Nell

———◆———

THEY WERE GONE. She was on her own. Rough elbows, hairless legs, clogged sinuses, chapped hands, aching back, upset stomach gone. Dear knees gone. The whole was less than its parts again.

How could They compete? She was at the Greenhouse Health Spa with Mommy and Mo. ("Wonderful, we've planned a surprise for your birthday. I was scared crazy that you'd get furious and wouldn't go. Moms already paid. I was afraid we'd have to carry you up there on a stretcher. You'll hate it but you can get some rest. It's back-to-school for mommies.") Loose bits of body were everywhere and discussed day and night: fat ankles, puffy eyes, split ends, bulging pones, sagging belly, hangnails. The Greenhouse was a body shop for wornout parts.

Nell had come with a good attitude. Somewhere else was somewhere else. Mommy had suggested Bermuda but the beach was dead and had no birds and Nell might stay indoors. She picked the spa because it got results.

Nell remembered about the outside world. It was full of news. She had brought a book along, on the World, so she would fit right in. It was called *Earth, Inc.*, which seemed inclusive enough. It was full of coping words and she copied the best of them out and put them up on the mirror of her luxurious pale green room:

> *subjectively apprehending . . . synergetically comprehending . . . objectively articulating . . . conceptually coordinating . . . cosmologically organizing . . . pantheistically manifesting . . . schematically rationalizing . . . infinitely extending . . . rotatingly everchanging . . . innocuously accruing . . . comprehensively producing . . . inexorably integrating . . .*

The spa was pink, yellow, and green: pink rosebuds on green paper schedules, pink baskets of complimentary cosmetics, yellow pots of mums in clusters of dozens in the domed greenhouse around the pool.

Everyone came with someone. Mommy had her girls, LaNelle and Moselle. (And wished aloud for Vinnie and Minnie, departed souls, as a unit of five was better than a unit of three.) Regulars met each year in the session that was "theirs." Bridge clubs came; and old camp friends. But mostly your group was your kin. The newcomers were put together at meals and for breaks, so that they made their own group. These were a lawyer from Tennessee recovering from foot surgery, an art critic from New York losing a small wine belly acquired in the south of France, a corporation vice-president here as a part of an executive fitness program, and a strange woman in dark glasses whom Nell, at first, thought must be an alcoholic.

In the late afternoon, after all the workout sessions, you got together with your group and gossiped around the pool or outside in the walled-in sunbathing yard. At this time you were allowed to pick up the house phone and order all the iced tea or coffee you wished and it would be de-

182

livered to you: no calories, plus a vase of pink rosebuds, green cloth napkins, and yellow lemon slices.

Mommy knew the spa would rescue her eldest. "What you need, dear, is color. Color is what it takes to perk someone up. You can't get well living in some place that's as white as a sanitarium, isn't that right, Moselle?"

Mommy had smuggled in a tiny box of Godiva chocolates and rationed herself one every afternoon at tea time. "Just one. That can't do any harm, now can it?"

An optional activity was the early morning walk, from 8:00 to 8:25. It was the only thing you could do that got you out the padlocked doors into the light and air and traffic outside. Nell had elected to do this, and the shuffling woman in sunglasses went too. They walked together, as you had to follow the leader in pairs. Her name was Minuette and she was shy. When they stepped out, the group, onto the sidewalk, there was an almost involuntary move to reach out and hold hands, like kindergarten children.

The high point of the walk was a tiny bridge across a small artificial pond, which was a water hazard on a golf course. On the pond swam two swans—ugly birds whose undulating necks were too long, making them seem miniature monsters shuttling back and forth across their tiny flat Loch Ness—and a trio of ducks. Nell preferred the ducks to the swans. Ducks had bodies that went briskly along, paying no attention to their heads; swans had heads that snaked away on elongated necks, leaving their feathered bodies behind. Ducks sat nicely like decoys, all in one place, until the instant they overturned themselves to dive for food. A neat feat, with a sleek touch.

The women negotiated this piece of their environment with difficulty. It took most of the conversation of the walk: "Here's the bridge," "Look, the swans," "The water is bluer today." "Be careful." "Here we are." Nell felt at home. It was remedial conversation, first grade primer stuff. The bridge was hard for Minuette; it took all her concentration. She had to lower her head and clench her fists. But she could negotiate the language: "It's cooler today."

The busy birds, the regimented schoolgirl walk, her shy companion, all made the morning walk a special time for Nell. It seemed a maximum adventure for a newly pasted-together person.

Mo was vexed at Nell for leaving. "I can't see why you want to change clothes twice at the crack of dawn just to get a look at a third-rate golf course." They shared a suite, and morning was a time they could have had their coffee and confided lives.

"I'm Pantheistically Manifesting." Nell used her World words.

"I didn't think you would like all this. I thought you'd hate it. You were supposed to come to rest. Nobody does the walk and all four exercise classes. That's four hours a day. I just come so I can tell Maudie Farmer I've been and make up funny stories about it. You're the last person I thought would take it seriously."

Mo did not mind appearing poolside with makeup on, although they were asked not to, or taking a sunbath instead of a sauna, or skipping classes and bargaining for two facials. She had paid a lot of money, fifteen hundred for the week, and she felt entitled to do as she pleased. She felt that the six staff hands per customer were no more than her due. "People like rules so they can break them," she explained to Nell. It came out almost a scold.

Nell, face unfixed, hair tied back, gave her all to each

184

class in turn: warm-up calisthenics by the pool, water workout in the pool, spot reducing with weights in little rooms, spot reducing to music at the ballet barre. Calves ached and thighs knotted and shoulders firmed and stomach caved in to bring back Nell. All of Them, now Her, labored like little steam locomotives going up hill. They didn't, for one thing, have time or energy to slip away and hang Themselves up around the place. It was hard work; making a sum from all those parts.

She loved the singsong of the instructions to firm up:

Right leg up flex foot breathe out leg down point toe now again breathe in left leg up flex foot breathe out leg down point toe and again, right leg up . . .

In water class they moved hard yellow rubber balls in their hands, against their chests, between their feet and knees (dear knees). Forty-nine minutes that felt like patting your head and rubbing your stomach, and Nell could do it fine. Every day when she got out of the pool she had to laugh and laugh—how funny they had all looked paddling along like blowfish with strange yellow puffed-up parts forced down or out. Abbott and Costello Meet Yellow Ball. It was slapstick. Rotatingly Everchanging. Infinitely Extending.

"I thought you'd hate all this," Mo complained again, wanting them to sit in the sun, their feet up, and make fun of all this. "If you're such an enthusiast you could do this for two dollars a week at the Y at home."

"How is that possible?" asked Nell. "It wouldn't be back-to-school for mommies."

Everything was cared for; no part was forgotten. There were ministrations to Feet, Hands, Face, Hair. Parts were cut, conditioned, filed, buffed, fluffed, creamed, clipped, manipulated. Segments of Time were set aside for segments of Body. They were all earth worms divided into sections, annelids getting it together.

For Face she was taken into this dark room and placed in a sort of dentist's chair that was tilted backward so that her head was virtually in the lap of the technician. Her eyes were closed off with wet witch hazel; a towel turban muffled her ears. The attendant spread her face with a thick cream that smelled of Pepto-Bismol and left her for the better part of an hour. "Take a deep breath, that's it, the idea is to relax, now. That's peppermint today, doesn't that smell good?"

The pink and yellow and green place took care of them, piece by piece, and minute by minute.

From Face you went to Makeup, where Charles of the Ritz girls would draw on it: eyebrows, lips, cheeks. All about you would be gin drinkers and executives and regulars, offering up their sagging, ambitious, wrinkled, hopeful canvases for smiles and youth and beauty to be painted on. Nell did not like these sessions; they seemed to infringe on her specialty. (But then, she only painted Dresses. So they were not strictly in her union.)

Minuette was having trouble. She was leaning close to the magnifying glass they were each provided with, peering at the foundation cream and array of shades in tiny pots from which to chose a face.

"Did I tell you I just have one eye?" she whispered. "This one's glass."

"No," Nell felt that explained a lot.

"Yes, I was in a car wreck, you know. And then I got depressed and started drinking, and then I quit, and then I came here, you know, to get fixed up. My husband got tired of talking about it, and I was afraid to go out. I never left the house, because people would look at my eye. But my daughter thought this would help and she's paying for it. I want them to see me looking better."

Nell considered the woman. Her shoulders sagged and her thin stomach in its leotard sagged too. It was her spirits showing. Her neck was stringy. And on her scarred hurt face was a Charles of the Ritz pink mask: cherry cheeks, glaring white painted bags under her two disparate eyes, and a hard mouth uplifted in crimson over the downturning soft lips below. The daughter who was paying for all this, and the husband who was tired of it, would look at one another over her head and sigh. They would lie.

"Let me paint you, Minuette." Nell offered, turning her stool to face the grave woman.

"Minette. Minette Williams."

"Do they call you Minnie?"

She look embarrassed. "My folks did. But my husband thought it sounded country."

"I had an Aunt Minnie. She was a beauty. I'll fix you up to look like her." Nell said that to reassure; in fact the woman with the painted-on face already resembled Minnie far too closely.

She wiped the anxious woman's face with cream, and studied it. It needed a long white convent dress below it; a starched hat flying above it. She would do well as a nun, keeping silence, in retreat. Gently, Nell spread a light yellowish beige over the bare face. She mixed the shade from the colors on their two trays.

"Honey, I'll do that," the Chasritz girl in pink apron dashed over to prevent initiative. It was not all right if the kindergarten children crayoned outside the lines.

Nell cut her off. "That's okay." she said. "Sometimes its fun to practice on one another."

"We don't usually—"

"Yes, I know."

She left the dark circles under Minette's eyes, running a faint wash of light brown over them, letting them recede, painting above in the eye sockets a much deeper darker brown, until it apeared that Minette was a woman with deep-set shadowed eyes. She dusted powder on her light brows, making them fade away like downy face hair, removing any need for them to arch or sag. The dark eyes stood without emphasis. She colored the cheeks, which were soft and saggy, with a brownish rose, the color of dried sachet. She made Minette's mouth soft in the center, blurred at the edges. On the opposite side of the face from the glassy eye, she put a beauty mark, to balance its power.

"You look pretty, don't you?" She wiped her browned creamed hands on a tissue and handed Minette a mirror.

"I used to be," the woman said. "When I got married."

"Come join my family this afternoon for our tea party, will you? You can try out your new face."

"I always have coffee in the afternoon with the newcomers, you know. We have a group—" She hesitated.

"I'll tell my mother and sister that you are an heiress from Virginia. That your father owns tobacco and your dead husband had racehorses. They'll like that. That you had a daughter who died and you can't bear to talk about it. That way they'll do all the talking to cheer you up."

Minette made an uneven smile. "I don't look much like an heiress. But I did buy some new clothes."

"But here we're all in our tights and terry robes. Heiresses keep to themselves. They leave their jewels at home. They wear dark glasses."

Minette brightened. "Do you think I could do that?"

"Let's try and see. We meet by the pool at five. The far end."

"What is your name? I forgot."

"Nell. Nell Woodard."

"I'll try it if you say so."

By tea party time, hunger had settled on those who did not smoke. Snacks for the day had been four ounces of potassium broth, served at exactly ten o'clock (this made by cooking vegetables for twenty-four hours and then throwing out the vegetables and serving the hot water), and four ounces of a sweetish pick-up (a sort of Dietetic Orange Julius) served at three. The unlimited tea and coffee of the break was a jolt that tided the ladies over until supper time.

"We'll have one iced tea, one iced coffee, and one hot coffee poolside," Mommy commanded into the house phone. At other locations, the thirty-two other guests in their tight groups did the same. All still wore their work suits: green legs and arms, yellow terry robes to which were pinned pink rosebud-trimmed copies of the day's schedule. Mommy had wrapped a yellow chiffon scarf around her head and perched her yellow-rimmed sunglasses on top. She had on a few rings—nothing fancy, third-best jewelry, corals and jade—and some little little pink thonged sandals. (She had arrived with a box of color-coordinated poolside accessories for her visit.)

She complained that she had not lost an ounce and Nell did not mention the chocolates. She remembered Mo's saying that the rules were made to break. Mo, on the other hand, was starving herself in order to get into an Albert Nipon flowered dress that she had not been able to wear for two years. "I'm so hungry I could eat Priestley's pecker."

She groaned aloud. "In fact, I had to look twice at the son-of-goldfish we had for lunch to be sure that wasn't it. It's hard to tell beside all that sliced, riced, spliced, diced, iced rabbit food. I can't wait for supper. Salivate as you anticipate it: First course, water soup; second course, a lettuce leaf marinated in lemon juice; third course, two green beans cut into three thousand four hundred and seventeen diagonal pieces; fourth course, crouton of beef— no, we had that last night—maybe elbow of rooster; fifth course, twenty minutes of finger bowl; sixth course, eight- een-inch-high egg whites with Sucaryl and a mint leaf; and, seventh course, the smell of coffee."

Mommy waved that away. She wanted to talk about the trunk showing of Neiman-Marcus clothes. She had marked a beaded chiffon, which cost the price of a week at the spa, for a fitting in the morning. (To bring home a dress like that Mommy would have let Tommy dye his thatched toupee orange, or molest her daughters before her very eyes. Nobody's perfect; Mommy had her priorities.)

"I invited a woman from my morning walk to have tea with us today." Nell got her word in.

Mommy looked up. "Are you walking, dear? That's nice."

"Where's she from?" Mo asked.

"Virginia. She's in tobacco." Nell waited for that to sink in. Virginia still had the magic touch of Fine Old Family for those who grew up in border states. "She's very shy." She spun for them the story.

"I thought I was the one who picked up strays," Mo said, slightly jealous.

"Here she comes."

Minette had pulled her hair back with a scarf and was wearing her dark glasses. She looked quite mysterious and stark in her smudged brown and rose face.

With great ceremony, to show that the closed circle could be opened a crack, Mommy pulled up another chair, which was slightly outside the group, slightly jammed into the cluster of yellow mums, but still, they made a place for the heiress. She was Nell's guest, and it was good for Nell to get out and make friends.

"This is Minette," Nell presented her.

It was a pleasant half an hour. Minette was able to try out her new self, and everything she said seemed a confirmation of Nell's invention. "Oh, I grew up in the country," she murmured. And, "Oh, my daddy kept horses, but not really anything fancy. We just liked to ride them." "What? That's right. Times change. But I can't complain. You just get along the best you can . . ." "Here with your two daughters, Estelle, you're a very lucky woman." And then she slipped away, still in her dark glasses, as if she had had enough of the public.

Nell wished she thought the same act would play for the patched-up woman back home, but she doubted it.

It was Minette, and seeing that things were not going to change for her, that got to Nell at the end. She sat through cocktail time (four ounces of some stuff that tasted like pineapple juice and skim milk, and one carrot twist per person) and dinner. Next came the evening's entertainment (tonight a mystic, tomorrow, Bingo), which took place in the parlor with its Oriental rugs and bad paintings and brocade chairs, with all the women in caftans and second-best jewels. By then, Nell had had enough.

She took a swim in the cool green pool beneath the dome, alone. Voices from within filtered out to her through the network of closed doors. It was a good piece of time before the director counted noses, and located her. "We prefer our guests to stay in a group, Mrs. Woodard. We can't be responsible, you see, otherwise."

That sounded reasonable. Nell sneezed and went to bed. She wanted a little solitude. Mo would spend their last nights at mommies' camp talking into the night, for she was not eager to return to caring for her house and her position and all that went with the fall season.

What Nell wanted was a man. Too much of Mommy, Mo, Minette, the gang. No one spoke of a week without sex. No one spoke of men at all except to refer to them, as in: "I told my husband last week that . . ." No one said that all the exercise and dieting and preoccupation with the body were so you would not remember what its real needs were.

What woman who had an option would spend fifteen hundred dollars for a celibate week?

She lay with four eyelet pillows behind her head, a pale pink coverlet on top of her. She did not want to tend herself; her fingers, back when knees were around, had spent a frantic amount of time in her panties. She did not want to end her top-to-toe rejuvenation program at the Greenhouse in that way. What she wanted was a man.

Not Max (she could feel tears hot but not spilling as she made that painful admission), but someone who was *there*. She thought back to boys in high school who had wanted just to feel of Nell, who had wanted to undo her bra, who would have lived six months on the sight of her ordinary breasts just because they were breasts. Back to men before Max in Santa Fe; to someone she had spent time with, and then forgotten in the years with Max. A man who spent the afternoons loving her all over because he wanted her. It had been hot outside, red and hot because it was Santa Fe, and she had lain in his room, which was dark and cool. And he had kissed her back, and legs, and shoulders, and hips, and then turned her over and kissed her face and breasts and stomach and toes. It was all afternoon before he put his mouth between her legs. Nell, Nell, Nell, he had said her name over and over.

And what was his? She could not even remember. Where was he now? Loving some woman each afternoon, or spending his spare time on the golf course with the guys? It didn't matter: that was Santa Fe.

It was not wanting him, the nameless man, back again, or that time, or that place; it was feeling bitter because of all those years spent with a man who did not know she was there. Who said, "Did we do it? Tell me about it," at dawn, or noon, or the next day. Describe it to me. Give me fantasies. Fantasies of sex, the fantasy that we are having sex. Goddam it, Max, I wanted you. I wanted you every day and all night. I wanted you and you weren't there for me. You weren't even there for you. I did it all. It was worse than masturbating; I had to do it for us both. It was pornography and at the last there wasn't even a coherent audience for it. The man in the back row with the raincoat on his lap had gone home.

"I want some sex," she said to Mo as they were in their gowns sharing a bedtime glass of iced tea.

Mo stopped a minute, then plunged on, not wanting to seem taken aback. "You're missing Max, aren't you?"

"Am I?" Nell sat on the chaise facing her sister.

"They say widows do."

"Do what? Want sex? Miss their spouses?"

"Want it a lot. Part of that's the daily contact."

"Part of it is that you're not getting sex."

Mo looked offended. "But I mean if Max were back there you wouldn't be thinking that."

"If Max were there I wouldn't be here."

Now Mo was hurt. "Well, I'm here." She, who had two men back home.

Nell sighed—and lied. "I didn't mean it that way. Max was in no condition to be left. That's all I meant."

"I wasn't being defensive. I know you're hurting."

Do you? Does anyone know what it feels like for someone else? How can they? If we all had a glass eye and a husband who was tired of us, would we all understand one another? No. She used to say to Max: "I don't know how it is for you." And he would rouse and touch her gratefully. "No," he would say, "you don't."

(*I wish to God I never saw you . . . I wish you never came along with me.*)

"It's okay. This week has been good. It got me back together," Nell said. "It was time I was out and about, Inexorably Integrating."

"I didn't think you'd like it."

Nick

———

NICHOLAS SAT IN A MUFFIN SHOP on Harvard Square. He had ordered a blueberry and a bran, and talked with the waitress, a happy big girl from New Jersey who was learning to talk "like the Kennedys." "You got a quatah for some watah?" she showed off, pleased with herself.

Ostensibly his trip east had been to combine a conference with a colleague here this morning with a visit yesterday, via rented car, to Exeter to see his high school daughters.

The conference had been somewhat of a necessary formality, a trading of known information. The time with Jo and Joni at their new school and in their spotless room had been something of the same. They had toured him about on their long coltish legs, claiming him as their father; they had given him shy hugs in return for his stiff departing kisses. But they had little room for him in their lives.

The real reason Nicholas had come to Boston when the opportunity presented itself was to digest, away from home, a letter he had received last week from Maisie Cavender, sent to him by her executor two weeks after her death. It had been unclear whether Mrs. Cavender had intended to mail it herself or not. It was found in the lockbox with her will, which left everything, in Edward's name, to the clinic.

He had been so moved by her writing it to him that its contents had not yet sunk in.

He had decided to stay over an extra day, to look up his old college roommate, and mull the whole matter over in his mind.

He would have a muffin on the Square and spend an afternoon walking in the city, to get his bearings.

He liked to watch the students. It reminded him of the fervor of those days: to take a stance, to make a choice. He saw girls, women they were now, dressed as poets in black hair, skirts, stockings, and capes; and others who presented themselves as corporation material in short brown hair, skirts, and shoes. From his days at school he remembered students who molded their lives to project Empiricism or Rationalism. The story was that the first president of Harvard had been removed for his views on infant baptism; classroom courses told of fights that good men readily died for.

He did not miss it. Such thinking over-simplified.

Watching these students, his mind wandered to Richard, who had got himself written up in *The New York Times* two weeks ago, proving to their father that it was possible not to go to Harvard and still make it big.

It was a feature story on the idea of building a prairie from scratch; the point being that Richard Clark was no Goldwater farmer, but someone with degrees in organic chemistry and bacteriology, a prairie saviour who, as a child, had searched the railroad beds and old cemeteries for rare plants (an apocryphal story, Nicholas had observed, that part). There were photographs of the Reconstruction Habitat, as the tallgrass was now called, showing that this was no wildlife preserve, which did merely that, preserved what was scarce and dying out, but rather a vaster scheme: a plan to reproduce natural ecosystems in order to learn how the original ones had worked. The existing eight thousand acres grew slowly, the owner said, as seeds had to be gathered each year from scattered remnant prairies and refrigerated to simulate cold winter ground. Also, the land must be periodically burned to keep scrub growth down; originally a job, Clark explained, performed by Indians smoking out buffalo, or lightning storms.

(Nicholas knew what they had done with the Indians; but what had they done with the lightning?)

The article did admit that for the first few years a new prairie, even a Reconstruction Habitat, looked pretty much like any old farm on soil too poor and too sandy to cultivate.

It did not mention that the owner had taken to raising a crop of grass known as marijuana, a variant in the ecosystem, for his brother's former wife, who had a new lease on life due to its effects.

Nicholas did not want to think about Virginia, yet he inevitably did. She had been in one of the feature's photographs, a "friend" looking at a new shoot of life. And it had hurt him more than he would admit to see how animated she looked.

The waitress, scarcely older than his daughters, skipped back by, smiling a New Jersey smile, refilling coffee.

He left four quarters for her. He wanted her to remember him. ("Ears that stuck out? You shoulda seen last week. Paid a quatah for some watah.")

He got off the red line at the Boston Commons, and walked slowly up Beacon Hill. Through the windows in rooms lit inside even in the daylight, he could see bookcases, paintings, dried cattails, tapestries, children's art, racks of herbs. He imagined, against his better judgment, that all the people residing there were happy with one another. Inevitably, the narrow houses along the steep hill, with their warmth and the appearance of being well lived in, reminded him in some way of the Cavenders'. Here were places where moral people lived their lives. He was homesick for every house he passed.

At the top of the hill a young man was playing kickball with two boys in the bright chill air. Further on, an attractive young woman in a pink sweater walked along swinging a daughter by each hand, telling them something that made them giggle.

He envied them all.

He rounded a corner, and entered another world. Here were houses without windowboxes, chestnut trees, or children. Here was litter on the street, and some old rags and wine bottles in the gutter.

The street was in the shade and quite cool; impulsively he went inside a dingy café. There was a bizarre collection of people: each seemingly alone. An old man with blindman's dark glasses; a woman in orange rouge, wearing a shabby rabbit fur piece; a huge man, surely seven feet tall, with a large wide face, loose white skin, a tight black coat. They were all eating soup or having coffee. Sitting and staring.

This was the back side of Beacon Hill. The people who made the houses he had hungered for made these people, who also hungered. He shuddered at his likeness to them as he took his cup of coffee to a booth along the back wall.

On the walk back, he realized he needed to find a bathroom. He had walked around too long with too much coffee. He stepped into what looked to be a city college, or trade school, and went down some steps and through a hallway to a men's room. When he came back to the door he had entered, it was locked. He panicked for a minute, then cleared his head and found a uniformed watchman to let him out.

"Not from around here, are you?"

"Kansas."

"I could tell right off. I got a brother in Oklahoma. I'll tell you that story. I went to see him last year, the wife and I, hadn't seen him in twenty years, didn't have his address. But I knew the little town, so, well, sir, the wife and I just drove around until we saw this bunch of kids playing, and I said to her: 'That one's a Munger, I'd know him anywhere, that's got to be the brother's kid.' And, do you know, it was. Just like that. We called him over and introduced ourselves and he took us to his house, and there was my brother looking the way he ever did. What a reunion we had. You can tell family any place in the world, I said. And that's the truth."

Nicholas liked the story. He lingered a few minutes, explaining that he had come in to go to the bathroom.

The man conveyed that you had no business being out in a public place long enough to need what you ought to go home for.

"Thank you," Nicholas said.

He took the green line out to meet his roommate. Going west, the train suddenly came out of the ground and there were tall hardwoods and frame houses with deep backyards; crowded family places he had not seen as he rode in the dark underground. It brought a lift to his spirits to come out into daylight and the neighborhood of tended homes.

His college roommate, Claybaugh, was now a chaired professor of classics; he had made his reputation on the glory of Greece. Nicholas could not remember the name of his wife, whom he had known as a Wellesley girl, or anything about his children, although he knew from Christmas cards that there were some.

He considered what he should tell Claybaugh about Virginia. He could not remember if they had met when she came east. In his memory, his schooldays and Virginia occupied a wholly different time and place; he could not recall an intersection.

He got off the line at a train station in the midst of what looked like a small European village: bakeries, flower stalls, tea shops, a seafood market.

Claybaugh called to him from a small foreign car and they zipped off at once into streets with large old houses and tall old trees. The kind of rejuvenated homes that went with the little shops around the station. Claybaugh did not look the same. In college he had been a soft, affluent boy, with baggy trousers, good manners, and pleasant disposition. He was insular; and happy in his insularity. (Although to have said that was somehow as if you accused an infant *in utero* of being insular; Claybaugh was just in there, and liked the place.)

Nicholas smiled to remember; he had forgotten, with the deluge of time, how fond he had been of his roommate.

Now—it was hard to say what had happened to him. It was as if he still had money, but it was not buying as much. The car and locale, perhaps, but not what he needed to maintain that old feeling of security.

"It shouldn't be such a hassle to put an old friend up for

one night," Claybaugh said. "But Nat and I lead such separate lives now, and there we were upstairs screaming at each other about where the sheets were that fit the guest bed, and who should put them on. Preposterous. There are no servants; I forget that from time to time. You look the same, Nicholas. Not even much heavier. A few lines, but, what the hell, we wouldn't want to look like callow youths forever, would we?"

The house was a fine old place, painted yellow, with shingle roof, two stories, turrets, trees, and tricycles. (Tricycles? Nicholas was surprised.) He was glad he had come out; glad even that he had inconvenienced Claybaugh by making him deal with bedsheets.

Inside, there were two unexpectedly small sons. They said their greetings and goodnights with impeccable manners and were whisked off to bed.

Their mother said: "Hello, Nick, do you remember me? I was Natalie Collfield. I still go by that name, in my practice. That was radical when I graduated. You can call me Nat." She had his coat hung up, his body in a chair, and a drink in his hand before he could respond. "And this," she said, "is Parsons Abbott, she's a therapist with me. We work closely together. I wanted her to have a chance to meet you, as she knows all the threads of our lives, Clay's and mine."

Natalie seemed haggard, but quite attractive, and Nicholas assumed that what he saw as haggard was the current fashion of extreme thinness. He decided she had been one of the brown hair, brown skirt, brown shoe students; there was something contractual about her bearing. It did not seem conceivable that the sheets were not ironed and on their appointed shelf.

He noted that Claybaugh was Clay, she was Nat, he was Nick. He wondered if the visitor was called Parse. Time seemed to be of such an essence here in their life that names could not take up too much of it.

He shook the therapist's hand. Of course they would have fixed him up with someone. On some level he must have known they would; perhaps that accounted for his sense of expectation on the ride out. She projected the same competence as Natalie as she gripped his hand firmly.

"I guess the children were a surprise, weren't they?" Nat continued to do the talking. "I mean being such tots."

"Yes, I think I had grown them up in my mind."

"We decided, Clay and I, that we would wait to parent until my career was established. Until we could be sure that both job and parenting would be parity situations."

"How old are they?"

"Three and four. Men can never tell."

"They have good manners."

"That's for company. We feel there is a time and place for self-expression. In their rooms they can do as they like. Within limits. But we need to see to supper, don't we, Clay? Let these people get acquainted."

He watched through the door as Clay set the chairs up to the table, Nat put on the placemats, Clay set out the wine bottles, and Nat the glasses. That must be what had happened to Claybaugh—along with the baby fat he had lost the warm layer of protection between himself and the world. That must have been the hassle with the sheets; the guest room must have been his job, in the division of labor drawn up after careful consideration of what would be involved in the reproducing of their kind.

"You haven't seen Clay in almost twenty years, have you?" The woman, Parsons, asked him.

He realized he was alone with her and was expected to do something about it. You're the prettiest parson I ever saw, came to his mind, but he felt a stupid fool for even thinking of such a line. My work is going well, he would say, and then she would ask What is your work, and he would tell her, and she would Be Interested, or Nod Knowingly, as she was a therapist. It tied his tongue. He tried to remember how you looked at a woman your age who was a possible person to—deal with. He found that he didn't see her well. He got an impression of great out-goingness and general fuzzy outreaching outlines. Great God, he was muddling along like a fool. He felt himself going in instead of coming out. "Clay looks different," he said finally.

"How so? That's interesting. What do you mean? Phys-ically or in his manner?"

Oh, not all that. Nicholas sighed, and then smiled to cover it. "He's not nineteen," he said.

He was silent again, feeling that he had not given her anything real. What he had said about Clay was true and what he thought, but not the point of it. He wanted to ask: What is going on here? What are Clay and Nat for each other? What happened to Claybaugh and Natalie? And have her say: I think it satisfies them both. Or, they create success and that is what they want. Something on that order. Otherwise, there was no point in discussing the change in his former roommate.

He asked about her work with Nat, and as she answered he asked himself: What do I want? What do I want from a woman? He thought back to Mrs. Cavender, and how he had clumsily spelled out a question about history and sci-ence and she had said: But of course that is the problem, everyone comes to that. That was what he wanted. For someone to hear and make sense of what he said in her own life.

But how, behaviorally, did that translate? What could this pretty parson say back to him that would make him want to take his naps with her?

He could see that he was also failing her tests, whatever they were. It must be that her air of interest in him was an effort to elicit the same in return. She had shifted her legs and adjusted her skirt in a way that conveyed she waited for attention. Instead he offered to mull over her views on the trend toward family therapy.

He would like to have said outright: Let's don't do this any more. It's no fault of yours. You're fine. I just don't want it.

But she must have figured that out for herself for she excused herself and left the room (to help with dinner or check on the little boys or go to the bathroom and kick the wastebasket?)

They went in to dinner together to eat the meal that was jointly cooked and jointly served. Nat put the plates on, Clay took them off; Nat served the fresh fruit and cheese, Clay did the coffee and liqueurs.

Back in the living room he and Clay were allowed to talk about time elapsed, and paths crossed, and how it was then, and how they thought it would be, and how it was now. Parsons and Nat talked about clients, and trends, and stress.

"What happened with your wife—Virginia wasn't it? You said she wasn't with you."

"She left."

"Nick, hey, what a shame."

"No. She left some years after I wished she would."

"Hey, well, then, I guess you're feeling relieved about that?"

"More or less. After twenty years you hate even to lose a leak in the roof." (The line was not his, but he liked it.

It belonged to the watchman with the brother in Oklahoma.)

Clay looked startled and then laughed. "I guess so. You seem cool enough."

"She's run off with my brother." Nicholas had not intended to tell this, but having unsettled Claybaugh already, it seemed tempting to continue.

"No." A shocker, that was. "Your folks must be in a tizzy over that?"

"Makes for family gossip."

"Well, you never can guess—"

"My work is going well." Nicholas took pity and changed the topic.

"Hey, that's good. That's great. Mine is always uphill. The students never question the parameters of discussion. The department spends its time hiving-off into separate cliques that try to make big news out of their arcane specialties. I try to keep up with my tiny area, but don't always. It gets harder and harder to come up with good work."

It seemed strange to hear Claybaugh talk of internecine feuds in the department instead of the splendor of Greece.

"Most of the pressure," Claybaugh continued, "is because it's Harvard, that's what it gets down to. I'd like to say it doesn't make that much difference, but that's not true and never has been. You can count on one hand the persons that people have ever read who weren't here. I don't mean in your field—" He quickly excepted Nicholas, being, in fact, wholly unfamiliar with his work. "But in the standard fields. Dewey I guess is the exception. Not that I have such a high opinion of him."

"My father always said that."

"I met him once. Meant a lot to him, as I recall, your

205

being here in school."

"It did." Nicholas considered his old roommate. In school their relationship was such that it was his role to tell Clay-baugh that he was on the right track, was doing fine, had turned in a good assignment. Now he said, "It looks as if you've got yourself where you want to be."

"Sure, I have. In the department and here at home with Nat. It's hard to foresee all the problems that can come up, but I think I can handle them when they do."

It was clear that Clay was proud of the fact that he and Nat lead active, equal, productive lives.

As if on cue, Clay jumped up at a signal from Nat and went to help with the clean-up.

Leaving him again alone with Parsons Abbott. He tried in his mind to make a move. To see if she would like to drive him to the station in the morning. To suggest that she come into Boston for dinner, that he would stay over. To offer a late-night walk around the block. To get, at the least, her address. He could not. He looked at her again. It seemed to him that if you knew what you wanted then you had some chance of recognizing it when you saw it; but that if you were vague and confused, then you ended up where you did not intend.

His concern was, that having spent almost twenty years with Virginia, he would be unable to get outside the pattern, and so would spend the next twenty with a non-Virginia in reaction.

The woman in the facing chair crossed her legs and looked at him, full of interest.

"I am not much company," he said in apology. "My wife and I are recently divorced."

"I overheard. How long has it been? How do you feel about that?"

"Hostile, I'm afraid. Hostile to women." He stood up and looked away. To give her a chance to deal with that. It sounded odd to hear himself say that; it was Virginia's accusation of him. Until this trip, it would not have been his own.

"I'm accustomed to that. It's a natural reaction—" Parsons attempted empathy.

He did not sit back down. When Clay and Nat came in to check on their guests, he was still standing. "If you found those sheets—" He made a slight laugh to show there was no censure there "– I'll hit them. It was a grand dinner, but a day back at Harvard has worn me out." He shook hands with them all, and told the woman visitor goodbye.

He told Nat, who looked quite angry with him, good-night. And told Clay that he would make plans to ride in with him in the morning.

"I'll pick up breakfast at that muffin shop on the square," he said. "Good night."

Upstairs alone in a yellow room, on the clean sheets that had caused confusion, Nicholas got out Mrs. Cavender's letter. It might be he could never come to terms with it. His view of his mother having been formed too long ago to change.

It read:

> *Dear Nicholas,*
> *I have become worried that I might die and a few secrets with me. One of which concerns you.*
> *If you can bear with my old handwriting, caused as much by uncertain hands as failing eyes, I will tell you what I know about your mother, as I have heard that you and your parents have been at odds since the day I saw you last. Some of it may be helpful to you.*

Marian Onderdonk was a patient of Edward's when she was at university. She had been accused by her family of drowning a half-sister in a pond on the family place. Her stepmother believed her guilty, and wanted her tried and sentenced for it. Her father refused to believe it and persuaded his wife to let the matter drop—with the proviso that Marian never again set foot in their house. In her grief and rage the woman, Olga Onderdonk, broke a promise to Marian's father, and informed the girl that she was not her real mother, and that she no longer considered her a child of hers in any way.

I enclose a newspaper account of the drowning; nothing of the accusation was made public. Marian was sent by her father to Edward for therapy. She had been very jealous of her sister, and had meant to be the remaining daughter to comfort her parents. The knowledge that she was a stepchild only, added to the accusations, drove Marian temporarily out of her mind. Although he got her into therapy, the father had, as far as we know, no further contact with his daughter.

After four years' work with Edward, the girl changed her name to Mary Ann Sargent (after the painter, I believe), and, as that person, met your father. I do not know what of this your father knows. Certainly nothing of Edward's part.

(Else he would not have invited him to dinner on that occasion when Edward lapsed into his old role, thereby making something of a scene. I forget—if he ever told—what he said to your mother).

Edward had some concern that you should know this, for he took a liking to you at once. I feel he would want me to write.

As to your estrangement from your parents: some-
times such breaks are for the best.

> *With affectionate regards,*
> *Maisie Cavender*

He could not take it in. He sat upstairs in this house of
his old, good friend. How could he have said to him; Clay,
do you think my mother did that? How could he have asked
the two efficient women therapists? They would have dealt
with case histories, not his mother. Alone, he tried to get
a new glimpse of an already impossibly tangled life.

Some things did make more sense for having the knowledge. Surely this explained the frantic attempt to get her
kinship with her family in print in the *Digest.* She must
have sought for a way to force them to acknowledge her.
She must have been exhilarated to learn that they were
called and her words read to them over the phone.

He thought her stepmother and two brothers were alive
at that time. He knew nothing of a sister. He tried to remember in her early wanderings some scrap of narrative
that mentioned "my sister and I, like you and your brother,"
but could not. He thought he recalled a time when she had
told Virginia and one of Richard's girlfriends a story about
a pond at her family's summer place. But he could not be
sure. That might be hindsight.

If she had not done such a thing, Marian, Mary Ann, his
mother, then the accusation must have been what jammed
her mind, making it go back over and over the point where
she had learned she was not the woman's own child. Stop-
ping there, unable to go farther back. If she were innocent,
how could she feel forgiven? Did not guilt and pardon
require others?

If she did do it . . . His mind balked. Then did that

explain the way she was? Did one do such a thing, and then go on in a world of her own invention, denying everything that did not fit the few safe facts?

He did not know. With the Cavenders gone there was no one he could ask. He missed them, and found himself holding onto the letter as if it were a part of them. Already he had unfolded and read it a dozen times—more for the presence of the woman who wrote it than for the message it contained. Maisie Cavender he had known; his mother he did not.

7

New Orleans

Nell and Nick

———◆———

NELL'S SON HAD A BROKEN HEART. Astilbe, who now lived with him as his sister was in love with his cousin Stein. This vicarious loss had been too much for Nell; she had relapsed.

Terry sent her to New Orleans. He had told Mo and Mommy that he'd asked Nell to look at a painting for him, one that the Bernais Museum might like to purchase. Nell with her eye was a natural for acquisitions, he had said.

He promised Nell that his friend Chelly—funny, old family, knew his way around town, good manners, a sweet person—would look after her. She was not to worry.

She had seen Alfred last week, in Terry's care. He had hardly said a word, but, slender, sandy, and upright, he seemed to be making it.

Mo had been ecstatic about her son, not knowing about the state of her sister's: "It isn't like Astilbe and Stein are really kin, you know. Tucker never adopted her, not legally. Yet she's in the family. You know the Friends are full of marriages like that—impossible for anyone outside to ever make sense of. Imagine, if they do get married someday, their children ever trying to explain who's kin to who. But she's a love. And everyone seems happy about it."

Nell sat in the hotel coffee shop, eating scrambled eggs and green grapes and grits. Still leading other people's lives, she eavesdropped on the liquid tones found only in New Orleans.

"Will you order for us, dear," a blue-haired old lady said to her companion.

"Ceecee said she'd be back in March."

"Is she physically able to make the trip?"

"She should get away. Her former daughter-in-law, she's still crazy about her, is remarried to a cousin-once-removed, and she's going to have a baby, and you know so often, at her age, there's danger. I didn't want to spread gloom, but I told Ceecee, I said, go to Paris and get your mind on other matters. She's a darling person. I'm sure she'll be fine. Let's have the batter cakes, shall we?"

Nell felt at home. Here, as well, families were all entwined with one another; and from time to time one of them was sent out of town to recuperate.

The news in the *Picayune* was familiar too: local stories laced with in-town names and gossip. She read of a scandal involving a man named Bobby Tibideaux who had let an asphalt contract to his mistress's brother. Skimming the words, Nell could smell the bougainvillea in a closed courtyard, see the lidded eyes of servants named Almost and Never. It was too much like home. She had come to get away.

She picked the paper for bits about what the outside world was up to when it was not among Friends. (Diane Keaton bought a fountain pen? Teddy Kennedy saw his child?) Two grotesque items soothed her spirits:

Here was a man who had been acquitted of murdering

his eighteen-year-old bride. He admitted to having sawed her limbs off, but said it was after she had accidentally died. The jury ruled excusable homicide. Nell sifted the distinction between those that were excusable and those that were not; it had the flavor of the highway warnings that said Stop Needless Accidents.

On the facing page was news of an inventor who was releasing on the market a Slumber Teddy Bear whose stuffing contained the actual sounds of a pregnant mother's womb. Not something she would buy, she decided, for her Babies Room.

She looked up to see a man staring at her. She had seen him yesterday in the lobby. The sort you know at once is a good man who would have a wife back home whom he was faithful to, and Eagle Scouts named Dolph and Rolf. She studied her seedless grapes. Why did she do that, assume banality? She had a son who was a good boy; he had a heart that bled when it was cut. She understood that sort. Maybe the man looking in the door had a wife he loved passionately who was a brain surgeon, and two grown sons on digs in Africa. Maybe he wasn't in this town alone having to listen in on little old ladies and comb the newspaper for strangers.

In the afternoon, Nell saw (on a street corner in the city of southern sin) the Salvation Army. Lonely staunch men and women singing for coins and the Lord. She imagined them beneath her pollarded trees, singing to the empty benches. She envisioned them in their uniforms, but with the women in flowered bonnets and the men in top hats. She could do hatted bands; you did not have to put a face on to keep your head.

She called Terry's friend Chelly, who told her that he had a wonderful scandal to share and to come out at once.

"My mother's cousin, Bobby Tibideaux, has let the cat out of the bag this time, dear, you can't imagine." Nell could. She told him: "I can't see you. I may go home. I may sit in my room until the weekend. But I can't go out. Terry told you I was in shambles? Yes, I'll call you if it lifts. I promise. When I can; but now I can't."

The next morning the man in the lobby was still alone. He looked in the coffee shop and decided against it. He went out the door, and she followed him: down Bienville toward the Market. It had to be all right to tag after. Anyone with ears like that could not misunderstand.

Nicholas looked up from the registration desk the first morning he was there and recognized the woman from the artists' table in Santa Fe, years ago.

She had on a dark cotton shirt and something twisted around her neck (beads or a scarf? he couldn't tell). Her hair was shorter, but something in the way she kept shoving it behind her ears was familiar. Maybe she had done that when she came up to the man at the wicker bar. He couldn't remember. But with more emotion than was appropriate, he remembered *her*.

He felt a lift to his spirits. The presence of this woman from the past seemed to say that he had a second chance. Not necessarily with her; she would hardly be unaccompanied. But her reappearance suggested that you did not lose for all time what you had done without.

New Orleans seemed a heartless city in which to be alone. It fostered an air of vice and immorality that made one feel a loner, a voyeur. Whether you put your quarters in the peek machines or not, it felt the same. He was tired of observing; he did that in his work. He did not want that in his life. (That must have been one of the attractions of

Virginia: you were dragged into her scenes and recriminations whether you wanted to be or not.)

Virginia, whom he wanted to be finished with, persisted in inhabiting his mind. He replayed their discourse and discord over and over. He could not tell whether this was to justify his having stayed that long, or whether it was because the space she had occupied had not been filled.

He had watched the woman from Santa Fe as she headed toward the elevator. She seemed wholly distracted, preoccupied, her mind elsewhere. He did not know why that was so attractive to him; he suspected it was because it implied an interior life that you did not have to supply, that could be shared with you. He recalled his negative reaction to Parsons Abbott in Boston, and his feeling that she had had nothing to offer him but himself.

He watched the dark-haired woman and wondered if she were still seeing the man she had left the bar with in Santa Fe; or if the thought of such constancy was merely an indication of Nicholas' own habits.

He took lunch alone. Neurochemistry had become an arena of competition; who could get a breakthrough and get it first. As evidenced at the conference, this had the same air as *The Double Helix:* a heated track meet. Nicholas had attended no sessions after he gave his paper. He did not want to participate in a race, and no one was ready to debate his work on other grounds. Margaret Ormandy, the British chemist, had waved at him across the lecture hall, but he wanted to be by himself.

He ate at a place he had seen from the street; it reminded him of the bar in Santa Fe. It had the same greenery and intimate air. Here, too, people talked in a shorthand manner, interrupting each other, calling out, making sense only to themselves. He wondered if these were painters, too. He had the idea that was how all artists spent their time.

The woman he had seen in the lobby did not appear. He winced at the thought that he had expected she would. That that was why he had chosen this place. Convinced that she would walk in firmly, a tall woman, look idly but not anxiously about, know several of the regulars, and then walk to her usual table. She would be at home in the café, but preoccupied, her mind on something that he knew nothing of.

He had crab, at an unbelievably high price, and then dessert, a meringue with lemon sauce and strawberries. It called for a cup of coffee, which the waiter, seeming to read the slight lift of his head, appeared with at once. The service was like the food: flawless. Only the company was wanting.

He could see that if you were alone for many years you would become particular concerning your meals. You would have the need to invest a great deal of time and attention in the quality of a sauce or a flambé or a coffee blend. If only to give solitary time some dimension.

The thought dismayed him—and he left, the dessert only tasted, the coffee untouched. He was not ready to settle for that, not yet.

The next morning he decided not to go into the hotel coffee shop. He would only be looking for the woman from Santa Fe, and what would he do if she was there, doubtless with someone else? He was creating a fantasy built on a long-ago scene, and he knew it; it appeared to be his pattern. But this city contributed to that. It pandered to its solitary visitors. One peek for a quatah.

He walked to the French Market and found that the little fried donuts were excellent, as was the strong chicory-based coffee. The place was jammed with tourists, guidebooks in hand, no different from himself: here to see the muddy Mississippi roll, eat soft-shelled crab, and appear not to mind when mascaraed men walked by in women's clothing.

He was talking with the waitress, a blonde girl in stilt heels, when the woman from the artists' table came in the door. He set his cup down to watch her pause and look around. She was in brown pants and a cream-colored shirt, and had the same thing knotted at her throat, a cord he saw. She pushed her hair behind her ears in a persistent gesture.

Then, incredibly, she walked directly to Nicholas' table.

"You're at my hotel, aren't you?" she asked.

"Yes."

"May I sit down?"

He nodded. He did not trust himself to speak.

"I've seen you in the lobby so I thought it would be all right to join you here. I hate to eat beignets alone. I hate to be in New Orleans alone."

He was constrained by her words. They seemed an echo of the conversation in the Maoist bookstore, when Margaret Ormandy had said to him: You looked safe, so I followed you. He did not want it to be the same again, not with this woman especially.

"You mind, don't you?" She jumped back up. "You meant to be by yourself, I'm sorry."

"Sit, please. It was too much to hope that you would join me, and when you did, well, I seem to have lost my wits. Stay, please. I'll get you coffee." He raised a hand.

She sat and looked around, not at him. "I have a secret wish to be a waitress," she said. "They like their jobs."

"I have secret wishes about them." He made an effort to relax.

She laughed, but guardedly. "You're sure I'm not intruding? I followed you from the hotel, but then when I was here it looked a forward thing to have done."

"And I made it worse." He pushed in her direction the plate of hot powdered donuts. "My name is Nicholas Clark."

"I'm Nell Woodard."

"I've seen you before," he told her. "It is odd to have your name."

"Oh?" She looked disappointed. "You'll turn out to be a friend of ours, won't you? My sister's lover, perhaps. And we will spend all my time here talking about the family and friends. I wanted a stranger, desperately." She frowned, then smiled slightly, as if at a joke. "Not that you look Mo's type—"

"It was Santa Fe."

"Oh?" She looked away, her face suddenly closed. "There were so many people there. We saw so many all the time. I'm sure I don't remember. Should I? Were you a friend of Luciana's? She had a man, whose ear—"

"It was in the Blue Parrott bar, in nineteen seventy."

"A vintage year for Santa Fe." She seemed absent.

"You rescued my wife from a man she was picking up." She looked blank.

"He was short and red-haired. She had a halter on, and a tattoo."

She saw him now as if she had not seen him at all before. "My God. *You* were the husband?"

He nodded.

She tore a donut in half. "That was the night I saw Max for the first time."

"I was envious of you and the man you went away with."

"Me too. I was envious of them for six years. Don't be." She drank her milky coffee quickly.

"Was he important to you?" A clumsy way to ask it.

220

"He was. He's dead. Except to me, and I'm doing what I can about that. Lobotomies and grafts of one sort and another. Back home. I'm back home in Texas."

"Why are you here?"

She looked up and stared at his face. She was somewhere else. Suddenly she laughed and said: "Because my aunts kept bobbins in the refrigerator."

He did not understand.

"But you meant in New Orleans, didn't you?" Her tone was gentle.

"Yes," He had meant that, but now he would have preferred to pursue the other answer.

"Because I am escaping heartbreak." She stopped as if she did not know what to say. "My son's stepsister, Astilbe, with whom he is in love, is going steady with my nephew Stein, who is her stepcousin. In fact, Stein and my son Alfred are double first cousins, as my sister and I married brothers. But although Stein and Astilbe are more kin than kin, as my sister Mo says, because Astilbe was not formally adopted they can kiss in cars and nobody minds. In fact, everyone is glad. Except my son. You see—" She began to laugh as if she could not stop. "But of course you couldn't possibly figure it out. You'd have to be in the family to understand. Keep it in the family is the first commandment at my house."

"The First Commandment is the first commandment at my house."

"How strange." Nell smiled.

"*Stein* is an odd name, for a southern story."

"Oh, that's Stein of Frank and Stein. My sister's twins." She waited.

He did not understand.

She hunched her shoulders and flailed her arms, re-

221

peating slowly: *"Frankenstein."*

He was appalled. "But that's a joke."

"Names are inside jokes at our house."

That did not seem possible. He thought of his family. Richard Royce Clark, Nicholas James Clark: even in their midst, scholars had been planted. Wat Tyler, the dog, was a joke. "My brother Richard," he said, "would like that—"

She clapped her sugary hands. "Nick and Rick!"

He had to laugh. He had flinched involuntarily at her use of nicknames for them. "We come from different places," he said.

"We do." She seemed amused. "I don't remember you at all from Santa Fe," she said. "What happened with your wife?"

He told the story briefly, not going into detail.

"She left you? You must like misery." Nell looked ashamed of what she'd said, and added quickly, "I'm sorry. My mouth has not been itself these last months."

"What did you mean earlier, when you said that you were here because of an aunt's refrigerator?"

"The same way you're here because your ears stick out. Mommy would have hocked the family silver to pin them back." She smiled to soften the words. "And slept with the plastic surgeon as well."

He did not understand; but, on some level, he felt that what she said was true. He touched his foolish ears. He had not thought to ask why they were never fixed.

"Let's take a walk," he said. He feared that at any minute she would leap up and go, as quickly as she had come.

"Okay, but first I need to go to the bathroom." She stopped their waitress and the two heads leaned toward one another before Nell disappeared around a corner.

He did not know why her talking with the waitress

pleased him, or why he felt such anxiety when she was out of sight.

They walked along the river as she told him about San Antonio, parents incredibly called Mommy and Tommy, a sister whom she loved, more about her son. He tried to do the same, reporting on growing up in Kansas City, Richard, his parents, Virginia, his daughters. But he felt that he withheld most of what mattered. Some things would take him years to know how to tell.

He wanted to feed her. The French Market did not count, as that had been her initiative. He wanted to take off her shoes and bring her cake and coffee.

"Are you an artist?" he asked. "Were you, in Santa Fe?"

"That's what I do, paint." She slipped her hand into his. "What do you do? At first I thought professor, but now it doesn't fit."

He sketched his work, but could feel himself hesitate in the wake of Virginia's hatred of "the rats." He found it easier to talk about the Cavenders, and what they had been for him as a schoolboy.

"They're what you wanted to be when you grew up?"

"Yes, I suppose so."

When it was clear she was not disappearing, he coaxed her to the place where he had eaten lunch the day before.

"I looked for you here yesterday." He was embarrassed to admit it. "This is where I thought artists would come."

"It's not at all like Santa Fe," she said, surprised that he should think so. "Nothing. That had a perpetual sunset which glazed everything. This is southern green; a grape arbor in the summer heat." But then, looking afraid that she had offended him, she added, "But I like this. It reminds me of the aunts. I miss them. Vinnie died years ago; and then Aunt Minnie went to a rest home, where she spent the last six years of her life picking blackberries one afternoon on the hill behind the Springs Hotel."

"Vinnie and Minnie?" He could not get used to it.

"Yes." She smiled.

"The crowd seems the same as at the Blue Parrott—"

"Oh, no." She shook her head.

"Why not?"

"I'm not sure. They're all kin here. This is where you come to have rémoulade with the cousins. I don't know. It feels like home to me. My sister Mo could tell you. She notices these things."

He liked hearing her talk. "I'll take your word," he said. He liked the way she thought, and the way she sat in a chair, and the way she had walked down the street. It was hard to explain why he liked it. He tried to figure how she spoke or behaved that was different, but could not. Yet it was. He watched her most of the time. As she talked she sometimes reached out and touched his hand.

She enjoyed the lunch, and hearing about the conference and why he had walked out of it. She ate a lot, and he liked that too.

"What did you want to be when you grew up?" he asked her.

"Good," she answered seriously.

He wasn't sure what she meant. "Are you?"

"Sometimes. Sometimes I get up and look at it and it's right."

He saw that she meant her work, and was pleased.

"I have these trees now," she continued, looking across the room as she concentrated. "And they're right. I am going to do them with a Salvation Army Band. Twenty band members, one with a tuba, and the benches empty . . .

224

But sometimes, it's bad. There was a pink dress that washed down the drain. In Santa Fe, when I got started, it wasn't good."

She talked about how she worked, and he strained to catch each word; he had heard none of it before. At first as she described the process of her art, he thought it bore no relation to his preconception of an artist standing at an easel looking at a still life. Then with a start he saw, in fact, that was precisely what she did. You were misled by the fact that what she described in such detail was the *construction* of the still life; the *painting* of it she seemed to take for granted. It made him rethink his assumptions. Perhaps Cezanne spent fifteen years arranging fruit and apples, and painted them in an afternoon?

He wanted to tell her that what he did was in the same way as radically different in its approach from the traditional view of laboratory research, yet as literally a repetition of it. He hesitated, but he needed to try: "To use your terms, that's what the rats are for me; they are a model I build of an idea that I see in human terms." He felt awkward trying to articulate such a matter.

She pushed at her hair, and looked excited by his words. "I never thought of science like that. All of us must do the same thing, Nick. We must all have the same idea, and our hands pick different things to build to say it. So it looks different; but it starts the same. It must be the way every kid asks: 'How do I know I'm not dreaming,' and—"

Nicholas jumped half out of his chair. "Every kid says that?"

"—then when the adult says: 'Wake up and smell the cocoa,' you stuff it back inside and forget you asked, or think you do. But all those things you wonder about when you first look around, and what you see doesn't make sense the way they tell it to you, stay in there somewhere."

Nicholas felt as if he could cry. This woman had dismissed a lifetime of living with the pressure of being the elected son in an elected family. My God, he wished his father had been here to hear this. He wanted Nell to say it again, in the same way, to his father. If every kid on the block asked that, then you did not have to be the one to find the answer. If every child in school wondered these things, then it was fatuous and deluded of your parents to imply expectation in your case. If every boy and girl dealt with appearance and reality over Wheaties—

Then they could get the prize. Richard could get his picture in *The New York Times*, and it would do for both of them.

By suppertime they had already wounded one another. Nell knew what that meant. (She remembered Max saying: You've been sullen and castrating, you must be involved.)

It had been over the children. They were standing by a gray Victorian three-story house—camellias and crepe myrtle and magnolias pressing the spiked metal fence that was designed to keep strangers out and kin in. In the side yard was a playhouse, a tiny exact replica of the big house. Nell had stopped to watch as a Dress floated under the trees hanging with Spanish moss and came to rest beside the gray Victorian child's house. It was a nanny dress, high-collared and in command.

"You should eat in one of these old homes," she told Nick, who kept wanting to provide meals. ("I want to feed you cake," he had said and kissed her on the sidewalk immediately after lunch.) "I came here once with the aunts to visit cousins. We had ham with a sweet apricot glaze, sweet potatoes with brown sugar, fresh corn that had been cooked in sugar water, and the fresh peas, too, little caramel buns and sweetened tea and coconut cake."

Nick was tall—her head came only to his chin—yet he held himself back, stooping, as if not to intrude too much of himself into the space around. The skin on his face and hands was stretched tight and had some sun spots, not as dense as freckles. The thing that struck her most was the way he didn't move. Max had been a dervish: always pacing, changing shirts, talking, showering, pacing. This man seemed to do all of his motion within himself. It was as if he never shut off the motor inside and so had to conserve his body's energy.

She could not shake Max off. She kept going in her mind back to that afternoon in Santa Fe, that feeling at the start; the couple in the Parrott, going off with Max, taking him inside the white room, the feeling of having found him and being so sure about it.

This man, Nick, she had not even seen. He had not existed for her. What if, instead of Max, she had gone to the bar and taken Nick away from his slut of a wife and the drunk who was enjoying her? How would that have been? It would not have been possible. She knew that, for she knew that girl, Nell; her elbows and knees had never come loose.

It made her draw back from Nick, as she could feel the same thing come over her again; she had found someone to care for and she wanted to go at once up to the room with him and pull down the shades and take off her clothes and start over.

More than anything in the world she wanted to start over, not do it all again. What if she loved Nick already? In his moral, groping way he could break her heart as thoroughly as Max. Although it might take longer; he was slow.

Even as Nell had told Nick everything about her life, returned his kiss, held his hand on their walk, her mind kept flashing back to Nellie Melba, to the Home for Lost Boys, to the deceiving feeling that This Was It.

She wondered about Nick and his daughters. She was vulnerable to daddies. She asked him how they got along, still keeping her eyes focused for security on the nanny dress beside the gray playhouse.

"Not well," he answered. He told about a recent trip to see them at boarding school. To him it seemed so little. She, who had not had even that from her father, wondered what the high school girls had felt inside, watching this stooped and caring man turn to go.

A question came to her out of her response to him and his wishing for more from his daughters. She asked before she thought: "Are they yours?"

He frowned. "Not really." He answered slowly, pondering his words. "They were Virginia's from the start. I had little part in them growing up. She and her two sisters were raised by a grandmother—her mother died when she was born and her father left—so that she grew up as part of a threesome. And resumed it. At least that is how I explained it to myself."

She let him finish, and then said carelessly, "What I meant when I asked if they were yours was: yours or your brother's?"

His skin went white. "I misunderstood."

She felt instantly guilty. Why was she hurting him? "I shouldn't have," she apologized. "My mouth has been recalcitrant for months. It just came out. I am not always benign. It was unkind."

228

"No," he said, "it was a fair question."

But it was not. She bit her tongue in anger at herself.

They started back. She thumped the fences with her fingers and talked about the homes. A lot of them had playhouses, but only one had had a nanny dress.

She told him about Chelly, whom she was supposed to look up, and how they would never have met if she had. And that led to who Terry was, because she could see Nick assumed a lover, and how Terry had looked after Alfred, and what that had meant.

"Is your son gay too?" He asked her.

She drew away and looked at a magnolia tree. "Would that explain Astilbe?"

"I was getting revenge."

"Were you? No. You wouldn't do that. It's what one would ask."

"Please, don't. I was striking out—" He looked undone.

"It's all right, your asking. It might even be all right if it were so." But she didn't mean that, and felt shame that she didn't.

They had been more fragile then; walking back to the French Quarter, holding hands, breakable as glass. Blows exchanged, then weapons hurled away. That happened, Nell remembered. Vulnerability set in. So did panic. She did not know if she was strong enough to bare herself again.

She took him to eat dinner in the back room of an old house, which had a fireplace and a chandelier with real lighted candles. A wind had blown down the river to chill the spring night, so the flames gave warmth of every kind.

After a rest and fresh clothes they had walked the streets, had oysters and drinks, mingled with the crowds having anisettes and ramos gin fizzes, listened to the jazz of Sweet

Emma's Band through the open door of Preservation Hall, seen the female impersonators, and listened to the sidewalk barkers describe the girls with rotating tassels.

Here they had white wine, and soft-shelled crabs and scallops, and hearts of palm, and, for dessert, a sweet cup of flaming chestnuts and ice cream. An almost all-white meal. She had forgotten how good it felt to be out to dinner with a man. She wanted to linger, to stay in this elegant seclusion until they snuffed the candles and the fire went out.

Over dessert they talked of love past. It did not seem so frightening with the wine and flickering lights and the whole day behind them.

"How was it with Virginia at the start?" she asked. She meant in the bed, and also in his head and heart. She could not be sure he did not still want what he thought himself to have found the first time.

He told a painful story of a grandfather and women with butterflies etched on their tender breasts. She could imagine him, this good man, a guilty lusting teenage boy not knowing where to go from there.

She was gentle as she brushed away his effort to accuse himself of therefore mistreating Virginia. "I don't believe that. Maybe you told yourself it was the tattoo, so you could rationalize taking her from your brother. But I bet if she hadn't had one it would have been something else. Nothing is that easy. I know I told Max that first time that he looked like my father. But I know that was an excuse I made up for picking up a stranger in a bar. I don't know what it really was. I don't think you ever know. Or could do anything about it if you did.

"It's like the fairy tale where the witches cast a spell on Sleeping Beauty that she'll prick her finger on a spinning wheel. You never doubt that; even when her daddy banishes them all from his kingdom, you know she'll find one. I think the spinning wheel is there. The butterfly was your excuse for not being able to avoid it."

He looked happy at her words. "In the bar in Santa Fe I thought you were coming to get me—"

"I asked myself all day how it would have been if I had."

"I was afraid in the Market that you would walk past me again."

"That wasn't possible." Either time, either place. She believed that. She did not know what she had been telling herself with the spinning wheel story; maybe that she did not have to run from this, or play that it was not taking place.

"How was it with Max?" Nick asked in return, although it looked hard for him. "At the start?"

"I don't know. I told myself it was perfect. But in fact most of it was my invention. When he was on the coast and not in Santa Fe I painted all the time, pink-washed dresses, tattered matters, an apprenticeship. When he was there, I gave myself over to him completely. It was, no doubt, as much a fantasy as yours—"

"Why did we do that?"

"It was the only way to get work done, I think."

"Don't say that, Nell."

"No, let's don't say that." She reached across to touch his cheek and sandy hair. "Let's say we took what we could find."

Nick rubbed his eyes. "When we had fights about this, Virginia called my work a sublimation. For what I should have been providing instead."

"I hate that word, *sublimation*. It's what you do when you have no hands and so you paint Christmas cards with a brush in your teeth."

"I hate it also, because it suggests work is what you do only if you're not good in bed." He flushed slightly.

"People get angry, and they hurt where they can. Nobody can do two things at once. That doesn't mean whatever you are not doing at the moment doesn't matter. If you are taking off your clothes, you can't be painting." She reassured them both. She wanted it to be all right.

He ordered brandy for them.

She let the lights flicker in her eyes, and thought of the sound her fingers had made dragging along the wrought-iron spikes of the fence in front of the gray Victorian house, like thumping the pads behind piano keys.

They talked of things they had done as children. He told of sledding down the hill. She told of Sears and Roebuck paper dolls.

"Do you like this place so much," Nick asked. "Or are you scared of what comes next?"

"I like this place. I like being out at night. Having dinner out. I couldn't do that with Max."

"I was thinking that Virginia could not have stood to be in this room alone with no other diners, not even a mirror."

"We don't let them go, do we?"

"We seem not to."

"I don't want them with us any more."

"Nor do I."

She took his hand and put it on her face. It felt dry and hot. Maybe even inside his hands something worked all the time. "Maybe we can leave them here," she whispered. "He'll be drunk and she'll be making ready to show off her tattoo when the waiter comes, and they won't see us go—"

They kissed in the elevator, and again outside the door of her room. She touched his ears. It was another world, his, the not being vain. How his wife must have used that.

She went into the bathroom and left him waiting on the bed. Would he still be sitting, fully clothed, when she came out? She was happy. She was going to take her clothes off and make love with Nick and he would be there.

She had worn for the evening a black skirt and a silky black top with blue and green birds on it. (She had brought it for Chelly. Terry said absolutely no brown pants in New Orleans.) It had seemed the nearest outfit to the London underground to wear for Nick. Now she had asked that they come to her room instead of his. She had planned a surprise.

Carefully, carelessly, she painted—with eyebrow pencils and eye shadow and lipstick brushes and lip glosses—a fine array of butterflies around her breasts. On this one, the left, which she could do best, she did four with wings outspread, delicate wings of greens and blues, and tiny black antennae. They were lovely. And on this one, the right, which was harder to negotiate, but she looked in the mirror to guide herself, she did four more, primarily pink and red, brighter colors to make up for the slightly mussier detail. And they were lovely too, with half-closed wings and long antennae. She studied herself: Erotic. She had never done this before, decorated her body. (Although she had described it once to Max, had thought of his waking to find her covered in tiny birds and flowers. But with daylight, and then afternoon, and fatigue, and anger, she had let it go. Had showered the idea away.) Now she was finally doing it: painting herself for love. She looked in the mirror and touched her breasts proudly.

"Nick?" She opened the door and went out to him naked but embellished.

He was on the side of the bed, in shorts and unbuttoned

shirt. She went to him and showed herself. She kissed his hands and put them on her.

Nicholas froze. He could not believe it. What had he said about his grandfather's story tonight to make her take it in this way? She had misunderstood; she had thought that he had to have that. He stood up in dismay. "I didn't mean this," he said. "I didn't want you to do this, Nell, please. I wanted you and not some copy of a schoolboy's tart."

Hurt, she stepped back and covered herself with her arms. "I thought you'd like them."

"You had no need, Nell." He was at a loss. "It was you I wanted."

"This is me. Especially me. You don't understand. I never did, I never had—" She got her black blouse and put it on. "I thought you'd like it." She put on her skirt.

"Don't be upset, please. Don't go away. I was afraid you had taken what I said wrong."

"I did butterflies. That's what you said the women had, butterflies. These are little butterflies with little wings and everything." She put on her shoes. She was crying. "You should have stayed with her."

"I didn't mean I didn't like them. They're beautiful." He was distraught. The fact of her being an artist, and what that meant that she had painted herself, had not dawned on him. He tried to hold her.

"You didn't even look at them."

"I didn't want you to think you had to do that, that I had to have—Nell, don't go away." He had been afraid of doing wrong; and he had. Even her gay friend would have known what to do with the art, even if he didn't know what to do with the woman. He would have talked about the customs of body painting in ancient Egypt or some such. Nicholas felt acutely jealous. It could not be of the unknown homosexual. It must be that when she had paraded out, so incredibly seductive, he had wondered if he were a substitute. "I'm afraid I thought you were thinking of Max," he confessed.

"I made a fool of myself." She cried motionless on the bed, her hands in her lap. "I was showing you—not just the butterflies, but all of it."

"And I didn't see."

"You couldn't. You were looking right past me at Virginia."

Was that true? Had he reacted against being asked to admire? In his mind's eye he saw Virginia let the strap of her lavender gown fall down, trying it out to see if the effect worked; he saw years of that scene, repeated without variation, in the grim purple bedroom.

Nell crossed her ankles and locked her fingers and squeezed her eyes shut. He thought she might disappear. "We said we wouldn't let them come up here. But we did." She sniffed.

He sat beside her. "We probably will again."

"I hate it. It feels like I'm a puppet and somebody is jerking my strings. Do you think that every time we have sex that there will be twenty of us there? Mommy and Tommy and your mom and dad, and Daddy, whom I can't remember, and Virginia and Max, and my son and your daughters. All those legs and arms and wide-open mouths?"

"Let's talk about it," he offered.

"No. That's all I did the last years with Max, talk about it. Make it up for him and me. I'm sick of talking about it. I want it mute for about two dozen years."

"I don't want you to take me wrong—"

"Take me wrong. Let me be a London whore. Make up

any movie you like. It's somebody else's turn."

"I want to see the butterflies," he said.

But she shushed him and turned off the light. She got his clothes off, wadded them down under the covers, and shoved hers down to the bottom of the tucked-in part with her foot. They were naked and in the dark. She kissed him until he forgot his anxiety and thought only of her.

He held her tight as they began to love. I wish we had done this in Santa Fe, he thought, no matter the reasons it would not have worked. If we had done this in Santa Fe, I would not have lost those years. I wish you had wanted me then. I am so grateful that you want me now.

"I love you," she said after a while.

"Yes," he said, "I see."

She laid her head on him and kissed his neck and he put his hands on her hair. He could feel her heartbeat gradually slow down.

"It's like playing the piano or riding a bicycle," she said. "You don't forget." She touched his face. "Now there won't be a time when we haven't done it, so we won't freeze up again."

To show her he had heard her, he pushed the covers back and began to touch her again.

Afterward he said: "Let me see them."

She turned on the light and they looked down. The colors were smudges. "They're gone," she said. There was hurt in her voice.

"Do them again. Bring your paints out here and do them."

"Are you sure?"

"Please, do them."

"Well, wait here then. I can't while you watch." She was gone into the bathroom with the door closed.

236

When she came out she had a bathrobe on. "You go, and then I'll show you."

She was waiting for him on the bed, on her knees on top of the covers, with nothing on but the tiny beautiful drawings. He was touched that she had done it again. This time he studied each one, talked about it, which he liked best, how they differed, which colors were the finest. That one, the pink and blue. There, on the left breast.

She had rouged her nipples also, and he took note of that, and touched her to show that he saw.

"I shouldn't have got mad," she said.

"We both will again."

"Why do you say that? You said that before."

"*Again* with you is more than anything what I want."

Nell sat desolate and perplexed on a couch in the lobby. What had he thought? What had she said to make him so mad? Did he think that she could be taken up there to his mother and father, and presented as: "This is LaNelle. I picked her up in New Orleans; she's looking for a waitress job." What had he expected her to do?

She had been so happy. It had been so wonderful. The walking and talking; the butterflies and not talking. She could eat dinners out and walk the streets and have someone in bed who was there, and who woke up with you. Nick. She thought of him and everything about him was good. And I'm Good with him, she thought.

She had saved to remember onto canvas the Salvation Army band, and the gray nanny dress. She was also working in her mind on a tattooed lady. She would be a fatty, with fatty arms and fatty thighs. She would be a torso beginning at a string of beads, with a skimpy shimmy that

237

showed a heart above the bend of each elbow, and ended in a dove above each dimpled knee.

"You said you loved me!" Nick had shouted in anger. They were to take a joint limousine to their respective planes within the hour.

"I did. I do."

"What does that mean?"

"What do you mean?"

"Translate it into behavior," he said.

"We did. We did it all."

"And that's it?"

"We can see each other again. You said we would."

"When? Where?"

"I don't know. Sometimes. We can work, and then, when that's reached a place—What if we work for six months and let this be there, and we can write, then we can get together?"

"Six months?"

When they had cooled down, they tried again.

"Why couldn't you paint in Kansas?" Nick asked.

"What is Kansas? Kansas is a word like sublimation. There's no such thing. It means Dorothy and the Wizard of Oz. I was in Kansas one time, in the train station, with three men in beards, two ladies with shopping bags, and one nun. I could paint there. But that isn't where I'd be. Where I'd be if I went with you is at your house. In your town. With your family. You'd be gone most of the time, and that would turn you into Max for me. And I'd be waiting, and that would turn me into Virginia for you."

They were in the lobby where they had first glimpsed each other four days before. It was full of flowers, real and painted, foliage, iron gates, urns—some attempt to combine a French palace with the Garden District. A small hotel, it

238

had a constant crowd. One more couple fighting made no difference.

"You said that no one could do two things at once," Nick insisted, his skin stretched tight and his tall frame sagging, "but that it did not mean that whatever you were not doing at the moment did not count."

"That's true. So we can do that: work, and then see each other. What did you think, Nick?"

"That this would make a difference."

Nicholas did not want to have this fight. What had he done to make it happen? What had he misread this time? Suddenly, as they were ready to leave, Nell had acted as if none of it had happened.

Six months she said. Was he to take that and live with it? Send her postcards signed: Nick and Rick? (He did not want to think of his brother even tangentially. It made him feel that Richard in the same situation would be bringing this woman home: This is Nell, folks. This one I found in New Orleans, and she's a prize.)

But he was Nicholas, and he was not. He was upstairs in the hotel, staring at his packed bag. It seemed a repeat of all his misunderstandings. He never saw them coming in advance.

He sat on the side of the bed. He felt as though he could not now or ever change anything, make anything happen. It must be that he had always felt this, been on the side of this bed, but that it had taken Nell to make him see it. What you were at the start, you were at the last. There was no reprieve. *Predestined* was the word.

When he stepped from the elevator, she threw her arms around him. "Nick, I'm sorry."

"So am I."

"I love you. I'll write. I'll come visit."

"All right," he said.

She was in the brown pants and cream blouse she had worn to the French Market. He could see her again come through that door and walk directly to his table.

He put her in the waiting limousine.

He would take a cab to the airport; or catch a later plane.

8

At Home

Nick and Nell

S H E D I D N ' T K N O W what she had thought. That she could leave it behind? That it had not happened? Things were at a standstill. Army Band and Nanny refused to play and tend. Tattooed Lady put on a kimono. Nell had forgotten the point: You can't love what is not there. You can only love your memory of it, which distorts, and blurs, until all that is left is you. Love Lost is looking in a mirror. What did she have of Max but her own past fervor and grief and anger? None of Max.

She called Nick. "I'm bringing my big coat from out of mothballs." Taking to Kansas her brown overcoat from the Kansas City train station. "You were right," she told him. "We can't wait six months. We could be killed by Mack trucks, fall off the edge of the earth, marry other people, have amnesia. I'm coming up."

"How long can you stay?" She could hear the panic in his voice at getting his wish, out of the blue on a Tuesday.

"Forty years," she said and hung up the phone.

Nell arrived at her future in the old long brown coat, her hair held behind her ears with combs, and a thick brown scarf around her neck. She looked out the airport window into the Kansas City night. It was snowing, like in the movies. Everywhere fine white snow, littering the cars and taxicabs and people.

The people were out of the movies too, oldies of years gone by. They wore gored skirts and animal-skin furs and those things on your feet (galoshes? rubbers?). They reminded her of the old musicals where the hero with wavy hair and a big chest sings into the camera, and wins the spunky girl with the tight curls and the full skirt.

What was she thinking to come live in a place where the snow fell, and cows grazed, and railroads ran, and harvesters did their job, and industrialists foreclosed the mortgages and had wives in animal coats? She didn't know what she was doing.

"I don't know what I'm doing," she said to Nick, running to him and throwing her face against his.

She had been afraid she would not recognize him. It had been only forty-eight hours, but she was sure that she would look at all the waiting men and walk right past him. But when she saw him, the tight face, the thin sandy hair, the ears, the unconcealed pleasure at seeing her, she thought: of course. She touched his face. "I remember you," she said. She hadn't invented him after all.

"You are beautiful in your college coat." He held her close. "I could not picture you."

"I was terrified in New Orleans. I'm sorry."

"I am now." He stroked the coat as if it were her skin.

"We'll take turns," she promised. "It's snowing."

"What? Yes, this should be our last of the year."

"It's like the movies." She peered at his eyes to check the terror. "What happened to the Nick in Louisiana?"

"I'm afraid this is the one in Kansas."

At the old Muehlbach Hotel he registered them as Mr.

244

and Mrs. All about her was the past. The lobby swarmed with the finalists for a regional basketball tournament, a convention of heavily chaperoned Lutheran youth, traveling salesmen with calling cards, and couples signing in as Mr. and Mrs.

On the wall she saw a flyer for the Policemen's Three Ring Circus. Cotton candy and balloons and clowns and lions, and three tired elephants standing on two front legs lifting a girl in a tutu, and imitation Wallendas from Lithuania swinging in the air above nets, and little people piling out of cars—twenty at a time—and the poodles in ballerina skirts on ponies. All of it had played a long time ago. She could see where the past went: to Kansas.

"Nick—" she said, clinging to his arm.

In the room it was better. She took off her clothes and he knew not to talk, and they loved for a long time. Forty-eight hours had seemed as many months when you were not sure you would have it again. He touched where the butterflies had been, and he was no longer frightened; and she saw that he had thought he would never see her again and so made him new promises and gave him back all that he thought he had lost for good.

"Let's not show up tonight." She dreaded meeting his parents, whom she had begun to picture as Franklin and Eleanor Roosevelt.

"They're expecting us for dinner at six—" he said, as if that was all it was necessary to know. "They think we're coming from the airport." He looked embarrassed.

"They don't know we're here?" She looked around their red commercial room.

He hesitated. "I didn't want you to have to put up with separate rooms at their house; nor did I want them upset at the idea of our being in a hotel in the town where they live.

245

I told them we were driving on to Topeka after dinner."

"Are we?" Nell was touched that he had got the hotel for two hours only; that he had known they would need it at once.

"We can come back here if you want."

"I want." She rubbed his chest. "Let's not go there for supper."

"But I told them—" Nick sounded as anxious as a boy about to be late for school.

"At my house Mommy would love postponing it. She would have already had the fun of planning tonight, have set the table and chosen the plates and glasses, and planned the menu and laid out her clothes. The actual meal would be anticlimax. She'd be delighted to have us shift it to brunch. Then she could plan another table, switch the glasses, decide to make the fruit salad into a compote, and wear something gayer for morning. You see, we would be giving her two parties for the price of one."

"I can't do it, Nell—" His voice carried apology.

"Dinner at six at your house means Dinner At Six."

"That's it." He laughed a small laugh. "She doesn't handle change. She operates on such a—"

"We'll leave in thirty minutes." She rubbed him gently. She tried to imagine his house, his life with its unvarying mealtimes. In the winter months the same table setting; every Thursday in Lent the same menu. Grace spoken in monotone in unison. The mother, Eleanor Roosevelt, presiding in her triple strand of pearls: "More boiled beef, LaNelle?"

"I want to tell you about her," Nick said. His voice had got very low.

"I can see for myself."

She could feel him draw so far away in his anxiety that

she had to wrap her arms around his chest to hold him there.

"My mother isn't stable," he said.

"Oh?"

"I'm not asking you to make allowances—"

"Do. I will, when you come to San Antonio."

"But last year I received a piece of information that perhaps makes some sense of her behavior."

Nell waited, holding tight. She did not want to stop his saying what was bothering him so.

He told her about a letter from the wife of the man he wanted to grow up to be. As she listened to what Nick said she realized that he carried in his heart the horror that his mother might be a murderer.

Nell considered waterholes and sisters. She imagined Vinnie and Minnie at the mineral springs; herself and Mo in the river. It could not have been like that. She thought of Mommy and someone in her way. It could have been like that . . . But after all these years the dread event had already found its home, had settled into the person who had done it and become a limb of hers. You could no longer have the person without it. "It's done," she told Nick. "Whatever really happened, it's done."

"I can't rid myself of it. If she did it; or if she had to live with the accusation. It haunts me." His voice was tight, as if the words hurt.

"You've not had time to find a place for it." She stroked him. "I do witchcraft," she said. "I'll put a spell on the Russian mama." She told him about the time she, a small girl, had made a handkerchief doll to look like bad Tommy, with a piece of his hair stuck on it, and some ashes, and a dead fly, and buried it outside in the rain—with a needle through its heart.

Nick relaxed somewhat. "What did it do to your step-father?"

"Who knows? He left me alone, anyway."

He touched her hair and face. Then said: "We have to get dressed to go."

As she put the combs back in her hair and buttoned her big brown coat, he admitted: "I don't want you to meet them."

"So I see." She watched him fondly. "I'll feel the same when my turn comes."

Nell had felt anxious that she would seem too tall, her suit appear too mannish, her white shirt too thin to have nothing under it. Or her mouth and cheeks and hose too dark. She had come prepared for formidable persons in an overwhelming house.

What she found, was, instead, so harmless.

Nick's father looked just like Nick. Older, and thinner, but the same, except that he had delicate hands which he protected as he moved. He had received her warmly, saying: "This is a pleasure. Nicholas has never brought home a girl before."

"I'm happy to be here," she told him. "It's snowing outside."

She followed the men into the parlor. It, too, was not what she expected. No degree of money or its lack back home could have produced the room.

It had an old brown mohair couch, a chair of the same stuff, a smaller deep red love seat, a fireplace with a black hearth, an elderly lacquered black piece that served as coffee table, here and there little burnished writing tables and old parchment lamps, a scarred carved table, behind the big couch, which had nothing on it. Cases of books lined each end of the room; glass-fronted cases, the kind that had a louvered piece over each shelf so that you could unlock only one at a time.

On the wall to the right of the fireplace was a tapestry of a hunt scene—dogs riding to death a faintly discernible fox. The horses were black, the hounds brown, the fox, berries, and hunting coats a dried-blood red.

It might all have been priceless; or all have been rummage. Nell had no context from which to judge. (It looked most like a stage set of the drawing room in the old home where the detective assembles all the guests, to tell them who did it. Sherry there should be, in a decanter.)

As she looked about for some, it was offered to her. She accepted, hesitant to ask for anything that was not in sight. She crossed her legs to show a stretch of seemly hose, and watched Nick and his father.

She waited, not aware that she did, for a glance to pass between them, the nod or smile or gesture that would indicate what they were to one another. But the two men sat, not relating, waiting. Nothing passed between them. (How could it be nothing to be with someone to whom you were that kin?)

Of course. Each lifted his ears like a deer in the woods at the rustle of the mother on the stairs. As she entered, they rose to their feet in unison.

The father did the introductions. "Dear heart, this is Nell Woodard, Nicholas' friend."

Dear heart. Nell stared. This was not Eleanor Roosevelt. Not anything like. This tiny bony old woman. This person was ancient, from another century, and, oh, so much like the aunts. The color of Minnie but the size and wasted bones of Vinnie. She was in a floor-length deep red dress that covered all of her and might have been the stuff of drapery brocade some decades ago, but now was soft and thready and tugged and uneven.

"This is Mary Ann, my dear," The father said to Nell. "Let's be on a first-name basis."

"It's so nice, I felt I'd lost my firstborn, but then, Virginia still comes, but you know, there is this, one doesn't feel entirely, and then, now, but you look so, not like her, but the height you know, that is, my Russian mother, she wasn't of course . . ."

Nick and his father sat on the edge of their chairs. Nick's face was tight, resistant, as if to deny what was before him. His father's was passive and patient. How could that stringy old thing captivate them so? How Vinnie would have loved to hold court in such style. (Maybe she had; maybe she took the Louisville cousin from Minnie with no difficulty.)

The old woman was giving Nell an account of their recent trip to England. They had been somewhere, the royal summer castle or retreat, and the woman clasped her fingers together at the remembering, composed herself like a child stepping forward to give a recitation: "I thought, somehow, seeing that, the greenery, you know, it would be nice to be the King and Queen of an evening, sitting, we never did that, back home, for a spell on that balcony, where, it was so green, you could see the young men at Eton in the distance, playing cricket on the grass, we thought, you know, that we should find ourselves, but then, my father and his Russian wife, who was not, you look so like, had a place, which they never, although that table came from there, was kept there, the carving, if you look close, some marks, out where there were no servants, so, but it has been in the family ever since, and I . . ." The mother unfolded her hands and smoothed her skirt. "So, you see, travel brings you home." She looked up brightly.

Nell moved over by her on the small couch and patted her knee. She did not even stop to think. The woman's anxiety was so great; the resemblance to Vinnie so strong. "There," she said soothingly, "I understand. About the table. People go away, don't they? We have only things left in the end, don't we?"

The men sat stone still.

"Yes, yes," the mother said and her eyes overflowed. "Do you know about that?"

"I do. My daddy left me. When I was three."

"Did you—get another, dear?"

"A beast."

The paper-thin old woman did not even dab at the tears that rolled down her cheeks. "The table—"

"I had, rather the aunts had—" Nell felt a great need to tell her about it "—some bone china roses from Italy. They were white and very beautiful. I never got them. They were sold. At least you have the table."

"Yes, yes, do you know—about that?"

"I do."

"You look so like, it's a comfort, I kept Virginia, even though, she was so, is, you know, not a generous, but I couldn't bear to lose, another . . ." She twisted her rings. Vinnie used to do that. It meant she was speaking the truth and would have a headache for it later.

"Where did the King and Queen sit on the balcony?" Nell gently brought the mother back to the story, going on before an answer was needed. "Kings and queens must never lose anything, don't you think that's true? That's how you get to be one."

"Did I tell you? Brighton by the Sea, Indiancastle, there were, you know, Chinese things, a room for jewels, what do you, the tombstone epitaphs?—"

"Brass rubbings."

"Yes, you never saw, and, of an evening, I should think, the young men at Eton, playing in the grass, so green you can't imagine, you never saw, such *things* . . ."

"I love your carved table," Nell turned and looked at it. "And it's yours."

The woman blinked and her face was dry. "Are you having dinner with us, in the spring, well, it isn't really, but so near Easter, we have fresh peas, the boys' birthday, my Russian mother—"

Nell bent toward her, almost touching her cheek to the old woman's hair. "It's all right. I've come to stay."

"One has to, one tries, it is hard to be sure, yes, I have often—"

The father rose at the shadow of a maid in the doorway. "Take my arm, dear heart. It looks as if supper is ready." He bent down to give his inclined elbow to his wife, and, for a moment, Nell could see her: bride, in a white dress, nothing under it, no body, no substance, no past, just a dress going down the aisle on the arm of a man who carried her as protectively as his own hands.

(Who was the father that he so badly needed this apparition?)

At the dinner table Nell said the aunts' words to them as they came to her. Admiring the place setting, and the crystal behind glass in the breakfront, she said: "It's so fine that you haven't put away your collectibles." And nobody laughed at her, and no one looked a glance at one another. The old words from that Rose and Red and Blue house in Mineral Springs worked equally well in this shabby narrow one.

The mother had skinned back hair like a rest-home patient, tight and thin, scalp showing through. It seemed a penance. The aunts would have died (and had) rather than be seen like that, would have had a wardrobe of wigs.

She saw the pond in a different way; and saw also that it was too late for her to put a needle in a handkerchief heart. The Russian stepmother had driven a spike through this threadbare doll at least a century ago.

She had not thought of the Capodimonte roses for years. It had angered her when Minnie died to think of everything in that house being auctioned off to the fey son of the mad antique collector—the roses probably being assessed by the pair of them high, bought by one of them low, and on their way to some fine home in Frankfurt or Versailles or Louisville. She had wept for them. Had remembered Vinnie twisting her rings, and Minnie saying she was no corpse yet. It did not matter; she had painted them. (It mattered a lot: she had lost them.)

She felt happy. She would see his house and find in it what she needed for her new life. They were headed down a gray road to the town named Topeka, where he had a job. Snow-smudged silos and barns and rolling land went by out the window. It seemed to Nell pig land and not cow land, but she was not sure how she knew that. She wondered if her tattooed lady would turn out to have pigs instead of doves above her calves. (Sties above her thighs? She smiled at that.) This place would change things. This light was what she thought of as winter light, which had nothing to do with the wet cold weather, but with the steely quality of the air. It might be here year round. Dresses once turning pink in the sun would silver here.

She felt relieved that they had dealt with Nick's last secret. He had loved her all night, as Mr. and Mrs., in the hotel, for her ease with Mary Ann. In New Orleans they had told each other the worst there was to tell; lying close together side by side the last night there. She had whispered to him about pink Tommy and the panties and he had become rigid, angry, disbelieving at the idea of a stepfather's fingers on a four-year-old.

But then, he had told her about the time Richard had left the tortured dog for him as revenge for his engagement to Virginia. And Nell had been appalled. To kill something that could not help itself. She could not comprehend the cruelty. How could he ever set eyes on his brother again?

"I don't know," he had said. "When you're in the situation—"

"Yes," she had said.

One gets used to one's own messes.

She hoped the time in San Antonio would go as well. Maybe Mommy and Tommy would flatten to nothing before Nick, turn into paper dolls.

"Sooner or later we will have to deal with Richard," Nick said now, his mind apparently also dealing with future worry. "I hope not until Christmas."

"Maybe we can go away for Christmas," she said. Enough would be enough by then. "Go back to Santa Fe, together."

At the suggestion, Nick took the steering wheel in both hands.

"I forget. Christmas is Christmas at your house."

He laughed at himself. "It will take me a while," he said, reaching out a hand to her. "I can't believe you're here."

"You were scared when I really came."

"You move very fast."

"And you are slow." She reassured him.

They drove in silence into his behind-the-times town.

254

Nell looked at the silver light. She invited the Salvation Army and nanny to come see. (As she watched, the green band uniforms turned olive drab, and the playhouse weathered to a slate. It would be all right in this new place.)

Suddenly Nick braked the car in the middle of a residential street. "I see my brother, as usual, has taken matters into his own hands."

She looked at the row of snow-topped houses with sloping roofs and smoking chimneys. "Where?"

"That's his car, the Volkswagen; in my driveway."

Nell tried to think what that would mean. "Will Virginia be with him?"

"I have no idea. This may be a solo welcome for you."

"Do you want to turn around, go to a motel?"

"No. It's my house."

She could see his face, set and walled off and hurt in a way she had never seen it.

As they got out of the car, she saw a dog on the porch and froze. She was terrified. Someone who could do that once—"Look," she said.

But he had seen the cur.

"How can you bear this?"

"I can't." He shrugged and walked as if he was in his sleep. He stumbled up the three steps to the porch of the clapboard house. The dog, a mongrel, brown and white, whined and cowered. Nell thought she would scream and run. She held his hand.

"Oh, shit, look," came from within and the front door was flung open. "Sorry, we thought you were gone for the day. Not that Mary Ann ever got anything straight in her life. I was getting these dishes, Nicholas, the blue ones. Do you mind? I know I said you could have them, but we needed them, and we were down here. We've been in the car with that damn dog of Richard's, Wat the What, and we need a bath, so I was going to grab the dishes and then head for a tub. We're staying with the folks in K.C., but I don't guess they thought to mention that. They do all this whispering around, as if we never heard of each other." The buxom woman in tight jeans and red t-shirt looked past her former husband toward Nell. She was a slippery sort; her gaze did not make contact. "This must be the girl-friend," she said. "Come on in. Don't just stand there like a stick, we're leaving."

"I thought you no longer had a key." Nick's voice was flat and stony.

"It turned out I did. Richard's. I know I left you one, but I forgot his. For God's sake, relax. A lot of harm I can do you out there in the pasture with a key to this bungalow. It's so empty anyway it looks like it's for sale. We've got the dishes; we're going. You'd think—" She shook her head, but did not look directly at either Nell or Nick. She kept looking around. For Richard? For what she had left behind?

Nell disliked her at once. She had never been able to deal with women who didn't like other women.

"Give me the key and get out." Nick stood on his front porch, talking to his former wife through the open door.

"For God's sake." Virginia flung something across the lawn into some bushes at the edge of the yard. "There. Go get it. Wear it around your waist. I bet you slept in your skate key." She hollered toward the back of the house, "Richard—The Prodigal Son is home."

A man slighter than Nick, better formed, with the same attitude of folded hands and convoluted ways of his mother, came into view. "Hello, there, brother. I'm ransack-ing your house. Pillaging the old place. Would you like to throw me out? I've never slipped through the door when you were standing in it before. A new scene. It seems we should do something. You could wound me in the leg with a shotgun. Or kill your ex-wife in my arms. Or—" He fastened his thin eyes on Nell, much as his mother had, but with a stronger undertow. (Here was one who could kill his kin.) "—you could introduce me and give me a chance to take one away from you, turnabout."

"I am Nell Woodard." She could at least do that, keep Nick from having to do that. "I've come to live here. Get that dog off the porch."

"Hired a Gun, have you brother?" Richard raised his eyebrows and looked more closely at Nell. "You had rabies as a child?"

"I don't like that dog on this porch."

"I don't like that dog, period." He moved briskly across the space between them, passed Nick, let the dog off the leash, and kicked it away. It went, tail between its legs, to stand beside its master's car.

"I told you this would be a hassle if we ran into them." Virginia walked into the yard, her hips moving in an exaggerated way from side to side. In the way of fat little girls trying to be provocative. The sashay worked: Nell was provoked.

"Excuse me, ex-. I've given you my excuse, ex-." Virginia laughed nervously by the car, waiting for Richard.

They drove off without the dog, and Nell felt ice inside her. But then, fooled you, at the corner of the short street, Richard opened the car door and whistled, and the hound lumbered gratefully up and jumped in.

Richard shouted at them: "When this one kicks off, I'm naming the next after Richard the Third. Who killed his wife and mother both. Maybe I'll give him to you."

Nell found Nick in the irregular wide hallway of his

257

house, and put her arms around him and said his name. "Let's walk all over the house," she said, "and get them out of it. Show me where you live. Where we live."

He knew it was absurd of him to expect another person to erase all of his painful past. Yet Nell seemed to do that. He had imbued her with that magic from the moment she met his mother.

He could not believe that she intended to stay with him.

He had eagerly agreed to have the long room off the living room (which was his former bedroom) painted white for her. "This will be a good room for working," she said. "It reminds me, with its windows onto the backyard, of the nursery at the aunts'. I can put my Roses here, along that wall, and my Eggs. And when you're home, it can open into the living room."

She had toured the whole house, and seemed pleased with its clumsy layout and oddly shaped rooms and spare-umbrella halls. "I like the window seats," she said, "you can set things on them, dolls, papers, clutter, pajamas. We'll sleep upstairs," she decided. "I like that. Upstairs feels like a place to sleep. Children do that in books; they say goodnight and climb the stairs. I've never done that."

In an afternoon, Nell had removed for him the bad memories from downstairs, and the old shutout feeling from upstairs.

He could not wait to take her to the lab. Although he had left the current experiments in his assistants' hands, where they would stay this week and the next until he got back from Texas, he wanted Nell to view them, certain that there too she would jolt him into reconsidering his assumptions.

At the clinic, in the hall, he introduced her to the man

who considered himself the competition: Jack Tovar, a research psychologist who would undoubtedly win the prize for proving what Nicholas had been working on all his life. Tovar's approach was imprinting. Six thousand quail eggs stayed in his incubators at all times, hatching out into chicks that stumbled through a maze of color-coded holes, falling, as programmed, into troughs below, and then, through another maze, into the final bins. It was an experiment set up to prove that if parent quails had been trained to feed at red light, then their offspring, even when bombarded with blue light from the instant of hatching, would head for the red light that to their "genes" meant food. Clear and direct proof—Tovar claimed in secret, careful not to let word of his project get outside the clinic—of the inheritance of acquired characteristics.

Nicholas hated the idea of this crucial point being made by ethology; Lorenz and his ducks, Tovar and his quail could only prove that you could stun the reflexes. The concept would be misinterpreted; put in a Skinner box, so to speak. (But that was the irony of his line of work: the psychologist would prove what the biologist could not.)

Nell looked in the dark room of flashing red and blue lights. She poked around in a big plastic garbage bag of cracked shells and unhatched eggs—those too small, too large, diseased, infertile.

When they were in his office, she said: "Link, rank, organize, subsume."

"Where did you get that?"

"From an article in the waiting room while you were getting me cleared for security. That's what you Fellows do in your program. Plus you merge with operations, drift with the trends, spill over into student lives. Link, rank, organize, subsume, merge, drift, spill over. I know about all that, it's called Synergistically Relating."

He did not understand but he liked having her there.

She looked out the window on the grove of trees below. "Don't worry about the quail man," she said. "He's just standing there painting by numbers. I think he throws in the Glad Bags all the ones that get it wrong."

"I haven't been worrying," he answered, as at that moment it felt true.

He showed Nell his hooked-up rats. And told her, in simple terms, about the chemical and electrical changes. Foolishly, he expected her, in her quick style, to lean down and switch over a certain implant—and make the answer clear.

Instead, she listened and looked. Which was in itself a breakthrough. He kissed her in front of the assistants. (In acknowledgment of his newborn expectations.)

Nothing in his life had prepared Nicholas for what he found in San Antonio.

He had wanted more than anything in memory to do for Nell what she had done for him: erase the bad and heal the wounds.

Instead, he stood in her mother's house, tongue-tied and immobile.

Seemingly unrelated comments that Nell had uttered now formed a pattern to him. He had been unwittingly forewarned, but had not known it.

"*Keep it in the family* is the first commandment at my house," she had said lightly, explaining the tangle of her son's misery. "I wanted a stranger desperately," she had told him, disappointed that he had seen her before, afraid he might be Mo's lover.

The woman called Mommy explained it in a rush when

they came in: "We didn't have Mo's husband Trey to meet you, and my handsome grandsons, because of course with the relationship which we're all thrilled over with Stein and the Smith woman's daughter, whom Trey's brother Tucker has raised, we would have had to have them too, especially, of course, as Tucker is Alfred's father. You can see that would not have worked. We're all so close, our family. Trey and Tucker are just like brothers."

"They are, Moms," Nell's sister noted.

"I mean to you, to us, dear. Don't be rude, Moselle." She turned to Nicholas. "I don't think about the fact that LaNelle has any connection with Alfred and Tucker, as an Artist is outside all this, and then something like this happens, and I think about it. And that takes care of it. Tell me, Nick, is it true you have a brother named Rick? I thought ours was the only family—"

There it was: *I thought ours was the only family.*

Tommy had greeted his stepdaughters with a pawing prurience that all took for granted. Nicholas thought with dismay that Nell's son might end up with the girl Astilbe after all—once she was his cousin's wife.

The only option here was incest.

How foolishly he had been prepared to reassure Nell that her family was nothing to worry about. (He had had the plastic flowers and caged birds of Virginia's Cleveland house in his mind. Nothing could have been farther from the truth: Mommy's house was a fine arts museum. There were indoor gardens at every turn, paintings on all the walls, the furniture had names. "These are Mies van der Rohe chairs, you know.")

"We have Perrier and Peñafiel." Mommy offered refreshment.

Nicholas had lost his tongue.

"That's two kinds of water," Nell told him in case he was not sure. "I wonder if you could find us some Scotch, Mother?"

"I'm sure, dear, we have some put away from last year, don't we, Tommy?"

The flabby man in pink shirt and green shorts trotted off obligingly.

"Do come eat, won't you? I've cooked all afternoon. I set the places in the small atrium, as we are only five."

She led them to a table on which was a plate of sliced breads, and four trays of raw vegetables. Nicholas recognized asparagus, snow peas, cauliflower, turnips, green peppers, carrots, and broccoli. He munched clumsily at a slice of dry bread that tasted of celery and cinnamon while he watched to see what the others did.

"Fibers." Nell frowned. "I forgot." She handed him his drink when it was fetched and got herself a plate.

When they were seated at the glass-topped table, Nell's sister told an anecdote to put them at their ease. It was about an event called the Texas Relays, where she had gone with her two sons: "We sat by these little white boys named Chad and Will and Christopher, and they were in their tiny Izods, and their daddies were talking about fettucini Alfredo for the party Saturday, and did it go, really go, with the trout with anchovy, would that do, and just as the runners hand off the batons for the first lap, the little boys say: 'Daddy, I need to tinkle, can I have some popcorn, I can't see, can I sit in your lap.' And over here in the same section are the little black boys in track shoes, named Bernis and Oliver and Khartoum, saying to their daddies: 'Pop that Soolie Boolie he pass it off slow to O.L. in the outside lane. Pop he slow today.' They know all the players, and the blacks they run their asses off on the last lap, legs turning like wheels, running they hearts out, and the little black boys they stomp and scream, and the whites decide that after all the fettucini is all right, and the little white boys have whined their way into large Cokes and popcorn. The blacks don't win every race, they just take first and second and fourth and fifth. So whitey wins third and that proves he's trying but he can't make it. And when the women run, the little boys and men scream their heads off for they sweeties. And the little white kids think it's the maids running. And their daddies are getting sunburned anyway, so it's time to go."

"Moselle, you exaggerate these stories. You didn't get that from me. That's the aunts talking. They could make a detective story out of a trip to the grocery store and what happened at the lettuce counter. I was always envious of that." She said this without much conviction.

Nicholas felt overwhelmed by all of them. He liked Mo because she was a smaller, rounder version of Nell, and seemed to dote on her. But he felt himself already pulled into the net, becoming a family tale: "One time my sister's beau, Nick, came down to visit, and . . ."

Tommy leaned forward in his golfer's garb to share with Nicholas the ins and outs about his income tax, and how he had deducted ninety percent of his gasoline, and all of his country club bills. Mommy pressed him about his parents and his brother and his house; he could tell her, she said, it was all in the family.

In a breather of silence, Nell said in a strange voice, "People used to drink Perrier and water in Santa Fe."

"It's healthful, you know," Mommy said.

"Moms, that was a joke."

He watched Nell eat a cold raw bite of broccoli.

Mo told another tale. "—So here was Terry shepherding

the Friends around, and then they flashed the slides that were the program, and it was Judy Chicago's Dinner Party. And here is Terry raving about the quality of the embroidery on the placemats, and Maudie Farmer is talking about the brilliance of the ceramics, and the ladies are craning because they are not sure they see what they see, and this old girl who must be ninety, she was once married to Maudie's grandfather, leans over and hisses in the ear trumpet of her neighbor: 'But, dearie, they all look like pussies to me.' "

"Don't be vulgar, Moselle. There is no need to quote such things out of context."

Nicholas could take no more. He felt he would get up and run out the door, except that he could not leave Nell behind. "Could we get coffee?" He lowered his voice and touched her arm.

"We have a Bunn Warmer." Mommy jumped to her feet.

"Sit down, Moms. Let him get his girl off in the kitchen by himself."

"Don't be coarse, Moselle. I want Nick to feel at home."

In the kitchen pantry alone with Nell, Nicholas leaned his hands and forehead against the wall. He felt sick that he could not do for her.

"What is it?" she asked.

"How do you stand it?"

"I go away."

"How?"

"Inside."

"Were you gone in there?" She had sat beside him, almost silent, but had not had the vacant stare she sometimes got when she was thinking hard.

"Yes. I could not bear to have them get to you."

"You think I'll turn into family?"

She looked distraught. "Yes," she said. "I do. It feels like no one can resist." She pushed her hair behind her ears.

"You mean that literally."

"Yes. You come close, and they get to you."

"I won't come close."

She sat in a chair and knotted her fingers, crossed her legs, and squeezed her eyes shut.

"I can't tell you it's all right," he said, full of remorse.

"Don't. It isn't."

"I wanted to."

"I wanted you to make them disappear."

"You can go to Kansas."

"Yes," she said and uncrossed her knees.

"Some things are clear that weren't before, if that would help."

"How bad they are, for one." She opened her eyes and studied a far wall.

"That you picked up Max instead of me because he would remain a stranger to you."

"Did I? I must. You looked somehow familiar in New Orleans. I thought you would have sons named Dolph and Rolf." She sniffled.

He pulled her to her feet. "That you left your son because it was the most you knew to do for him, to show him that one person at least could break out of this."

She wept.

Mo found them in each other's arms.

"Moms sent in the troops to get you."

"We're coming," Nell said, drying her eyes.

"Let's go out somewhere and eat. I'll call Trey. We could starve to death on Moms' roughage."

Nicholas shook his head. "It's time for us to go."

They made their goodbyes in the atrium.

Mo told Nell: "I'll almost never see you if you move to Kansas."

"Come visit," Nell said, giving her sister a hug. "It snows. Like in the movies."

"I forget about places like that," Mommy said. "I never think about them, and then when someone like Nick shows up from there, I think about them. Kansas must be like Missouri; I used to visit in St. Louis as a young girl with the aunts."

Tommy wrapped his stepfather's arms around Nell. (Nicholas saw there could be no guilt; it was in the family.)

Nell's son was there when they got to her house. Nicholas saw the pleasure suffuse her face before she said: "There's Alfred's car."

"I thought you weren't coming by," she said to the boy.

"Mo said I should."

"This is Nicholas Clark."

"How do you do, sir?" Alfred did not look him in the face, but he did not look away.

"Not too well," he answered. "I have come from eating at your grandmother's house." He hoped that would be taken all right.

The tall boy made a brief smile. "I got fed up with that years ago. At least you didn't have to go."

Nicholas felt awkward. He did badly with his own children; he had fled from Nell's parents. As her son mattered considerably to her he did not want to do the wrong thing this time.

He sat down inside, and the boy did too, while Nell fixed the coffee they had not got at her mother's house.

"Nell is moving to Kansas with me," he said to her son.

"Will you come visit us?"

"If I can. I guess I can."

It startled him to see a boy this grown think in terms of permission. (How easily his daughters, some years younger, had gone off on their own.)

Nell carried in a tray with coffee and cookies, which seemed to Nicholas—thinking of the Cavenders—a role reversal.

"Terry said you were fine—?" Nell looked at Alfred.

"He tried to fix me up."

"With whom?"

"She's married—"

"Oh?"

"Mo knows her aunt, Mrs. Farmer."

"Yes."

"Her marriage is rotten, but she's got little kids."

Nell sat on the edge of the couch. "You're young for that."

"Sure, but he was trying to help."

"Help both of you—"

"I guess so." He ate a cookie. "Did you think I meant fix me up with a guy?"

"No."

"Mo did, for a while."

Nell sniffled again as the boy drove away. "He didn't."

"What?"

"Maudie Farmer's niece. He didn't."

"That's good?"

"I think so. Astilbe was a sister, but the niece is still a Friend."

Nicholas shuddered. "He has you for an example," he said.

"I don't think it was me, I think it was the dogs. Red, Fred, Shred, and Teddy didn't belong to us; we didn't even know their real names. They were the only things he ever met he didn't already know. Fat Feddy was hit by a car." She wept. "He owes it all to her."

"You found the dogs."

"No, they found us. They came around." She took his hand. "You might as well see my pictures now. I can't put it off any more. I can't wait until they all arrive in Kansas."

"Why is it hard for you to show me?"

"Mommy and Tommy's was hard, but I don't live there. I've been gone from there forever. But upstairs in my room, I live there. So if you don't want that—"

"What must I do?"

"Don't say a lot. Don't tell me about them. You can touch and you can look."

She led him outside, then up into her studio.

He had also been forewarned about her paintings; but had not known it. She had told him what she most wanted to be, but, again, it had been in code for him.

He stared about him at a moral world. Everywhere were large canvases that showed a single white dress, alone in its purity. He could see that each, against its dark backdrop, represented Nell. The dresses had no faces, because the face was hers.

He touched each solitary virtuous version of her, as he went slowly around the disordered room. Early ones had an innocence that later ones did not, but he found the later ones more moving. The paintings of a dress (Nell) beneath a grove of ugly trees almost broke his heart.

Only in the ones in progress had she begun to do other people, if that was what they were. They might have been the dress disguised. He could not tell.

He saw a rough sketch of band instruments and hats. And of a shirt with one feathered sleeve. When he touched it, Nell said: "That was San Francisco."

Two of them were not white, but pink. Though as powerful, they were less appealing, more unsettling. In those, the background, which was also pink, blurred the outline of the dress. He asked about them.

"Oh." She looked across the room. "I did the christening dress when I left Alfred; and the evening dress after Max died. They bled a little, so I keep them at home—"

She looked at his face, and asked: "What did you expect?"

"I expected paintings; instead, they are you."

He felt tears.

She put her hands to his wet eyes.

"How *good* you are," he said.

Nell got her bearings in this half-house she was leaving. It had pleased her to see Alfred warm to Nick, who had been quite unaware of it. The same must happen with his girls.

She would miss the upstairs room, the walk, Vera and the café. The past.

She fixed a salad and Nick scrambled eggs. They drank more coffee, in her brown chairs.

She read aloud from the newspaper.

Here was a country couple who had lived together for seventy-five years. Ike and Ellie. They posed side by side in straight chairs, a settee and chiffonier behind them. They had got up every morning all those years at five, milked the cows, made biscuits, made children, lost crops. You could see it in their faces. Ellie told the reporter: "I was stuck on him from the start." Ike said: "She was the only sweetheart I ever had."

"I wish we had had that," Nell said. "Seventy-five years of five o'clock."

"I do too."

She thought of what they had missed, then; no longer of what she would miss. "I know we had to have been there to be here. But I wish we hadn't stayed there so long."

In her mind she painted Ike and Ellie: he in his stiff white collar, she in her white Sunday dress. They were good people, who loved each other best. You could see it in their Faces.

"I was stuck on you from the start," she said to Nick.

"You're the only sweetheart I ever had."

They lay down together on the Babies' Bed. "Let's take our nap," she said. "There's time for that."

SHELBY HEARON was brought up in Marion, Kentucky, and has lived most of her adult life in Texas. Her five novels previous to *Painted Dresses* are *Armadillo in the Grass*, *The Second Dune*, *Hannah's House*, *Now and Another Time*, and most recently, *A Prince of a Fellow*. She has also collaborated with Barbara Jordan on the congresswoman's biography. She has taught at the University of Texas, Bennington College, and the University of Houston. She lives in Austin, Texas.